DRINKING CUSTARD

First published in Great Britain in 2021 by Monoray, an imprint of
Octopus Publishing Group Ltd
Carmelite House
50 Victoria Embankment
London EC4Y 0DZ
www.octopusbooks.co.uk

An Hachette UK Company
www.hachette.co.uk

First published in paperback in 2022

ISBN 978-1-91318-374-5

A CIP catalogue record for this book is available from the
British Library.

Printed and bound in the United Kingdom

10 9 8 7 6 5 4 3 2 1

This FSC® label means that materials used for the product
have been responsibly sourced

DRINKING CUSTARD
DIARY OF A
CONFUSED MUM

LUCY BEAUMONT

Interruptions ~~INTRODUCTION BY~~
JON RICHARDSON

monoray

Deciding to have a child – it's momentous.
It is to decide forever to have your heart go
walking outside your body.
Elizabeth Stone

(Nice quote but you'd die if that happened, Liz.)

CONTENTS

I took my four-and-a-half-year-old daughter to meet some friends of mine the other day. We hadn't seen each other for a while and they asked how family life was going. I started to tell them that things were great and this was my favourite age so far – they're like your little mate but really they're still a baby. I explained how she seems too little to start 'big school' in September.

I was distracted mid-sentence as we'd reached a pond. I said to my daughter, 'Ooh, look at all the green slime on the top of the water!'

She rolled her eyes at me, glanced at my friends and said, 'It's algae.'

There was a silence. My friends looked at me and smiled sympathetically. This wasn't the first time I'd seen an expression like that on the faces of adults. In fact, I could write a book about it.

Oh. I have.

Dear Reader,

My name is Lucy Beaumont. I'm a comedian, a wife and mother. But not necessarily in that order. Five years ago, me and my husband Jon had our first (and only!) child. And along the way, I kept a diary of all my thoughts, feelings and ideas relating to 'the wonderful adventure of motherhood'. Now with Elsie off at school, life has calmed down a LOT and I've had time to look at what I wrote over that time and work out what actually happened over the last five years. Well, all I can say is – BLOODY HELL!

Becoming and then surviving being a first-time mum has been, for me, a bit like performing amateur pantomime on a rollercoaster. So much happened – if you're a parent, you'll know all about this – that it's hard to remember it all. So much of it is SO off the wall that people will never believe you. Or even worse, they won't be interested. Who wants to hear about other people's kids, eh?! Well, in writing this book I hope I've solved this problem for you. Just give them this book.

The truth is that parenting is random, unpredictable (apart from the completely predictable bits that everyone tells you will happen and you ignore them) and terrifying. And it is also joyous and very, very funny. And this is what I've tried to capture for you.

Now, I must be clear: THIS IS NOT A PARENTING ADVICE BOOK. Don't take any advice from it, as I have no common sense and have to lean on my husband for anything practical. If anything, this is a guide about how NOT to do it. In fact, reading these words back has been very useful to me as I've realized that I'm really quite odd and I probably should have relaxed a bit more. Then again, if I had done that I would not have got myself into some of the situations and predicaments that I present here for your entertainment!

Nothing really goes the way you expect in life, does it? And that's so true with having kids.

For example, my birthing process wasn't the experience I'd pictured. I'd envisaged a scene out of *Dr. Quinn, Medicine Woman* (if you are over 35) or *Call the Midwife* (if you're younger). You know, a woman in a white nightgown sat up, a sweaty brow, the vein in her neck pops up, there's a bowl of water (not sure what that's for?), she struggles a bit and huffs like she's trying to get a disposable razor out of its packaging and ppuussshhh…

Out comes a baby that is now on solid food looking for its real mother who is somewhere off camera.

Life isn't like that. As you are about to find out.

My husband, Jon Richardson, who is also a comedian (a better-known one than me), pops up in here every now and again. When I told him I was writing this book, he insisted he provide me with a glowing introduction. But then he couldn't stop and has written 'helpful' footnotes for you, lucky reader. I was in two minds about this! But in the end, I just figured that once this diary is published he'll read it and mutter away to himself about some minor 'inaccuracies' (I was probably just joking about something). And then I thought, maybe you'd like to know his opinions too! He *has* been a big part of this whole fiasco after all…

They say children teach you a lot about yourself, don't they? I think that's spot on, so I hope you enjoy reading this bizarre and eventful rite of passage. You never know, you might end up drinking custard too…

Lucy
X

INTRODUCTION BY JON RICHARDSON

Lucy Beaumont is a multicellular mammal of the species *Homo sapiens*. She has an acutely developed emotional response, which can lead to her crying at such images as a toothless man in fancy dress at a darts tournament, a gingerbread man whose head has broken off or a dog with three legs.

She functions best having slept uninterrupted for between nine and eleven hours each night but often finds this disrupted by loud noises, any caffeine consumed after 11am or a sliver of light escaping from a bathroom three houses away. She commits fully to each task she is required to perform to the exclusion of everything else. This means that while composing a text message she is completely undistracted, even by the approach of a jumbo jet spiralling noisily downwards towards our patio. Good news if you are waiting for a response to a text message, not so good if you are upstairs screaming, 'Lucy, for god's sake – RUN!'

In the short time I have known her, she has had no fewer than 11 new debit cards (the previous ten have all turned up later behind the fridge or hidden in the pocket of an old coat, now living a new life with several pistachio shells and a broken mascara). She is immune from any kind of hostage interrogation as she is usually so unaware of her passwords or the location of important documents that this information could not be extracted by any means, any more than you could find diamonds in a box of Shredded Wheat.

All of these things may lead you to believe that the unique hormonal onslaught of pregnancy and the sleep-deprived chaos of the early years of a child's life would have made our recent history incredibly trying. Luckily for you, that has been exactly the case and that is why you are holding in your hands a book full of hilarious stories that we look back on with smiles on our faces – now that the tears have dried and the walls have been replastered. None of it would be at all funny if Lucy was not also a wonderful mum. She is fiercely protective, uniquely hilarious and so upset that our daughter is growing older that she often offers to breastfeed strangers in the supermarket if they look a little tired.

These are probably the last kind words I will write about Lucy in this book as my job from now on is to make sure that the words you are about to read are factually correct. Where you see a footnote at the bottom of the page, this will serve as my melodic voice whispering in your ear to correct any inaccuracies or simply put my side of the argument where our perspectives differ. I will keep these to a minimum as you are about to enter the company of someone who, unlike me, people warm to immediately and want to be with as much as possible, which is an absolute godsend for a grumpy dad who doesn't want to have to go to birthday parties at weekends.

Jon

MY LIFE AS
A NORMAL,
SINGLE HUMAN
BEING BEFORE
EVERYTHING
CHANGED

Here is everything I think you need to know about me before you start to read my diary. I've tried to keep it brief as, let's face it, I'm not Elvis Presley. (You knew that, didn't you?)

I'm from Hull, a city on the north-east coast of England with a rich maritime history, full of warm-hearted, confrontational people. (That's a joke; they're unbelievable friendly and kind, honest!) Hull is famous for the band The Housemartins and Roland Gift from the Fine Young Cannibals. The former Labour MP John Prescott is also from Hull. He wasn't in a band to my knowledge but I once sold him a kettle when I worked in Comet, before someone threw an egg at him. And there are loads of brilliant women too, of course – like my mum, who's a playwright, Maureen Lipman, one of the best comedic actors of our time, and Amy Johnson who, in 1930, flew solo from London to Australia. Her statue can be seen outside of Hull's third-best shopping centre, exactly where she'd want it to be.

I lived with my grandparents until I started school and then me and my mum lived in lots of rented flats in a very 'bohemian' (rundown) part of Hull before settling in the suburb of Hessle, near the Humber Bridge. If you've seen pictures you'll know the Humber Bridge is like the Golden Gate Bridge but it's grey and not near San Francisco. Hessle was nicer than inner-city life – a bit rough at the weekends outside the pubs but nice, safe really.

On my first day at Hessle High School, the art teacher asked me if I would be rolling around on the floor fighting like my mum did, as she'd gone to this school too. She was a bit of maverick, my mum. She once dressed up as an old lady and wandered into assembly pretending to be lost and another time she got her uncle to drive his hearse around the playground while she ducked down with a white glove on and pretended to be the Queen. As you can see, she had a reputation that was a lot to live up to. In some ways, you could say I'm still trying to live up to it. (And failing.)

I had the best years of my life at Wyke Sixth Form College and I started working in Asda (that's not a sentence that has been in many books before!). I loved it there; it was like a cult. But instead of praising Jesus and sleeping with people, I hung around with middle-aged women and got 15 per cent off full-priced items. I took the job very seriously. Making pizza and cooking chickens is an art, I think. Well, it's skilled work. While others wanted to be on the tills or work in George, the clothing section, I took pride in putting on a hairnet and plastic gloves. I suffered for the role, though – I once got chased home by a big dog because I smelled of cooked meat.

And then a bombshell hit my mum. I left home!

I went to Hull University to study drama and I wanted to live near the uni, despite the cost, and it broke my mum's heart. She couldn't handle it; it was awful. I had to work late shifts at a nightclub to afford it, though I was only a few miles down the road. I think Mum was insulted and bereft. During my first few weeks at uni, she would ring me every night crying her eyes out. I know the bond between parent and child is strong but the bond between a single parent and only child is intense. (I've got a loving father, I've just never lived with him.) You really want to please your parent because, well, you're all they've got. At the age of 11,

I decided one day that I'd take all the child support benefit that we needed for a week's shop and go and buy a gazebo for our tiny garden with it. It took me hours to put it up, which I did while my mother was sleeping. I woke her up announcing that I had erected something that would help us have the best summer ever. When she came down to look at it, it had gone! A big gust of wind, we think. You can imagine that things were a little tense in our house for a while after that…

After university, I embarked on several failed attempts to live in London as an actress. Looking back now, what a shame that my mum stayed in Hull to be able to provide for me as I was growing up, and yet I buggered off down south the first chance I got! It was short-lived, though. Guess where the first professional acting job I got was? Back in Hull! I stayed in Hull after my professional stage debut and did some regional plays but the recession blew up and theatre took a massive hit. I had a string of jobs, including cleaner, youth worker, factory worker, call centre worker, nanny and waitress, and eventually I settled as an early years teaching assistant and loved it. I cried every assembly as the sound of the children singing made my soul weep with joy, but the itch grew and eventually I moved back down south to pursue a career as a stand-up comedian.

And then one evening a comedian friend invited me to go and see a comedy gig. I went and I met TV's Jon Richardson.

The rest, as they say, is history…

PART ONE

THE EINSTEIN MOMENT

I met Jon Richardson, the comedian, last night at a pub called The Fighting Cocks.

I'd been at a photo shoot for the poster for my Edinburgh show and afterwards, my comedian friend Tommy said he was going over to Kingston in Surrey to see a comedy gig. I went with him and, as I stood there watching the acts on stage, I felt someone's presence behind me.

I nearly fainted; honestly, my heart was beating like the clappers because I was sure Jon knew I fancied him. A mutual friend of ours, the incredibly funny Roisin Conaty, had told me one night that she thought me and Jon would make a good pairing: 'You're both northern, I think you're from the same village or something.' She asked where I was from, I said East Yorkshire and she asked if I knew where Jon was from. I replied that he was from Lancashire.

'Are they close to each other?'

'Er, not geographically,' I replied, 'but the War of the Roses was a long time ago now.' I couldn't help admitting that I had a soft spot for him. At the interval, Jon came over to ask if I wanted a drink. He seemed to know who I was; Roisin must have talked to him. I said, 'Oh yeah, just a glass of tap water please.' His eyes sort of widened – I think the Lancastrian in him was overwhelmed with adoration. I should have said a double whisky and coke.

Me and Tommy had to leave early to get the last train back home and Jon shouted over to us that we could both stay at his if we wanted – a bit creepy, but as we left the pub I had this feeling in my tummy that I wanted to turn back around.

We had our first proper date last night, two weeks after the comedy gig. At the end, something quite weird happened.

Jon dropped me off in his car at the train station and we swapped phone numbers. He gave me his number and I rang his phone so he'd have mine. Lo and behold, via Bluetooth, on his dashboard in big LED letters it flashed up 'MY WIFE'. I have never got out of a car so fast.

I rang my friend Jackie and she told me very calmly that he must be a psychopath and to leave London immediately and come back and live in Hull with her again. It must have been very strange for her – we used to sit and watch Jon on the telly in our 'slankets' (blankets with sleeves) and now I was getting harassed by him.

I decided that I should just ring and ask him what *the fuck* the wife thing was all about.

'Thanks so much for last night, Jon, it was really lovely food. I'll go back to his restaurant.'

'Whose restaurant is that?' he asked.

'Bill's,' I said

Jon paused for a minute, trying to work out if I was joking.

'It's nice to know where to get authentic Italian food from,' I continued.

'It's er...'

'Anyway,' I said, 'why did it say "MY WIFE" on your dashboard when I called you?'

Jon laughed and explained that Roisin had given my number to him at a party. He was very drunk and in a bad mood (I think that mood had lasted for eight years previous to that point, according to his book, *It's Not Me, It's You.**) Nevertheless, he took my number and put it into his phone rather presumptuously as 'MY WIFE'.

Ahhhh it all makes sense now...?

GETTING SERIOUS

I stay at Jon's house in Surbiton nearly every night now and have abandoned my friends and my little box room in a shared house in south London. Jon seems like the kind of person who will happily

---

* Jon – Still available online or in a charity shop near you, it's about my quest to find love as a misanthropic clean freak. I guess the fact you are reading this is as physical a spoiler alert as you can get.

visit garden centres and model villages. This is what I'm looking for in a life partner. He took me for a trip out to Homebase yesterday as he wants to paint his hallway. I noted there were four differently priced brands of masking tape available and Jon went for the cheapest. I thought that was a bad move as the cheaper they are the more likely they are to tear or let the paint soak through. I couldn't work out if Jon was just very trusting of the brand he'd picked or if he was tight. I decided he was tight.

It's good that he's tight: if this relationship is to survive I need someone who is going to be careful with their money and the money I haven't yet made, otherwise I'll just spend it all. And when I say 'spend it all' I mean I'll give it all away, in a charitable way but also in a way that means I just freak out when I've got money.

The things I'm looking for in a man have changed slightly from when I was younger.

TEENS: Does he have his own cigarettes? Is he striving to have his own car? Can he play football? Does he like hanging around on street corners? Is he funny?

TWENTIES: Is he in a band?

THIRTIES: Does he own a car? Is he funny? Will he look after my passport and national insurance card? Does he love his mother but not so much that she's smothered and can't go out with her friends? Does he like watching talent shows? Does he mind if I cry? Is he okay with the fact that I watch daytime TV up to and including *Homes Under the Hammer*? Has he ever missed an episode of *Location, Location, Location*?

You may have guessed from this that I can't drive and don't have any desire to. I struggle with lefts and rights and having to do more than one thing at a time, which they call multi-tasking. I hear a lot of men are scared of women using that word, but I can't do it.

Jon is kind, really moralistic and he's also a vegan. I've never eaten a lot of meat and dairy really and never thought of calling myself a vegan. But now I've decided I am one too. Jon says I can't be a vegan if I eat meat and fish and cheese and eggs, even occasionally, but it's no use, I like saying I'm one now.

Jon might be one of the best vegans I know because he adores meat so it's a massive sacrifice for him. He also really doesn't like it when I tell people he falls off the wagon a lot. When we go for a nice meal and they ask us what our dietary requirements are I say, 'Well, we're both vegans but Jon eats beef gravy and nice sausages* and I eat fish and blue cheese.'

It's not hard to be vegan. When you go out for dinner as a vegan and you've been looking forward to it for ages and you've bought a nice top to wear and booked your taxis and you say to the waiter, 'Have you got a vegan menu?' and he says 'No' then you just say, 'Well, I'll have a steak then.' The problem is the more I say I'm vegan that more I start craving steak. I never ate steak

---

* Jon – I do not eat nice sausages since sausages are one of the best vegan substitutions you can make. Even the arsehole of a lentil tastes nice, which cannot be said for cows. I am, however, embarrassed to note that I have, on occasion, licked my finger after sticking it in your gravy when I thought you weren't looking and I commend you on your peripheral vision.

before I became vegan! This seems to really annoy Jon.

I quite like annoying Jon. I think it's good for him. I wonder if that will become a problem?

Jon talks about meat a lot. He talks about the industry, the inhumanity and the contradictions of people who love animals but eat them and he also talks a lot about how good meat tastes. So when we go for a meal he'll order butternut squash and hate his life and everyone in the room. Why do so many places punish non-meat eaters with butternut squash? They don't seem to want to learn that vegans still want meaty, tasty dishes that fill them up. The times I've spent talking to restaurant managers about nut roasts and lentils and what herbs are and the times they must have waved goodbye and said to themselves, 'What a twat she was!' When I say restaurants I mean Harvesters and the ones attached to Premier Inns.

Anyway, when we go out to one of the restaurants I haven't already upset, I'll order a steak and then leave a bit and I say, 'Ooh, I can't eat that bit.' In silence, we'll then swap the plates across. I'm not allowed to look at Jon or say anything as he eats the last piece of meat and we swap the plates back again. The look on his face after he's eaten this piece of steak, after months and months of kale, is like...you know those videos that go viral of the little babies' faces when they get a hearing aid and hear their mothers talk for the very first time? Just like that!

PERSUADING JON

We've just driven back home to our home in Surbiton from the Lake District. It's lovely living with Jon in his house, even if Surbiton is not as exciting as some of the places I've lived. You know when somewhere's not exciting by how many outdoor things people can leave out. When you pass a house with wellies stored safely outside the front door, or a little bench, maybe a gnome or two, then you are not living in an exciting place.

I say that 'we' have just driven back. I haven't actually driven a car legally yet. I can do it, of course. I have driven the car with my mind. Admittedly, I have not been officially tested on my 'mind driving' to British standards but I have actually been driving ever since I was able to sit in the front seat – with my mind, keeping an eye out for hazards that the licensed driver may not see. I also like to control the music in the car and I like to have a nap and eat a pack-up. I'm a perfect driving partner, really. I will scroll endlessly through social media on my phone and then get very car sick and I may complain for a significant proportion of the drive but I will keep everyone in the car safe, as I have lightning reaction speeds and I make no bones about letting the driver know when he or she has just diced with death and how I have telepathically stopped it from happening. For me, being in a car is like a computer game: I am controlling it with an invisible steering wheel. This is why I can't drive yet and why people tell me to not bother. I don't care.

But anyway, momentous news to report. On this drive today, IT HAPPENED. On this very long car journey home, I think it was at a petrol station, I decided that, without any doubt at all, I would like to have a baby/child/affectionate adult with this man very soon. As soon as I thought it, I asked him. I knew it was a bit early to be talking about it so I trod very lightly. It's also worth pointing out that I'd got a cheese pie from the garage and it was giving me very terrible burps.

'Do you want to have a baby?' I asked. (Then I belched.)

'At some point,' Jon said. 'When we're married.'

'When are we going to get married?' (I held in a second burp.)

'We will eventually, won't we?'

'Yeah. When are you going to propose?' (The held-in burp escaped here. I think it smelled a bit so I wafted it away.)

'I don't want it to be a pressure.'

'Well, it is though, isn't it, if we want two kids? We're both 35.'

'I thought we only wanted one?'

'We might want two.'

'I don't want two kids; we both said we'd just have one.'

'Do you want a bit of cheese pie? It's repeating on me.'

'Can we save it for another time?'

'What's your problem with cheese pie?'

A NAPPY IN THE HEADLIGHTS

I can't stop thinking about having a baby. I think it's being made worse by the fact that we just got married; Jon's got a semi-detached house and a clean driving licence and I've bought a 12-piece cutlery set. It's all just fitted into place. We're like a couple in a building society advert so we just should be having kids. It just all makes sense.

I keep thinking about the box room I was renting when I met Jon. When I say 'box room' it implies you could get a single bed in there. No. My dad had to make me a bed to get one to fit but he decided to make it a similar structure to one of those decorating tables. In fact, I'd go so far as to say he made an upside-down shelf for me to sleep on. I've been looking at pretty pictures of baby nurseries today and I've found a thing called 'toddler furniture'. Did you know you can get special toddler-sized furniture?! Had I realized that then I could have got a toddler-sized bed, wardrobe and little dressing table for that tiny room. Instead of a weird shelf-bed, I could have saved up my £50-a-day teaching assistant fee and kitted the room out. All my life I've never felt the right size for things as I'm only five-foot-one and here I am, newly married and living in Surbiton, and I've only just found out I could in fact have put a child's writing desk in my old room when everyone around me thought I could only fit a single (shelf) bed. Actually, why didn't I just get a cabin bed? But then again, while toddler

24

furniture might have been better for me, it could have put off any potential normal-sized suitors.*

(It has just crossed my mind that by constructing me this strange rocking 'shelf-bed' my dad might have subconsciously invented a new form of contraception. So maybe it was deliberate.)

While looking at toddler furniture and thinking back to those carefree, M&S-reduced-microwave-meals-for-one days when I used to dream about sitting next to an open fire (or electric fire, as we only have eight years to save the planet) with a boyfriend who could play Spanish guitar, I also remembered a night around that time that might have kickstarted the whole journey I'm on now. It was such a special, spooky night but I almost forgot all about it. I don't want to forget it, though, I want to remember every detail of it because I think it happened for a reason.

It was three years ago now, a very cold November night, and I was on my way to a comedy gig. I was booked to headline and I'd performed at this venue twice before. I'd always had a good time so I wasn't as distraught to be heading out to a gig as much as I usually was.

Usually I was so nervous that I had no choice but to incorporate a handbag as a stage prop so I could put one quivering hand in the bag and the other on the mic stand. It took me a long while to work out that people then just noticed my knees knocking instead! I always tried to make it look like it was just part of my act that I didn't take the mic out of the stand but

---

* Jon – Well, you hit the jackpot there, then…

really it was so no one saw my hand shaking. These days I have a new-found respect and understanding for Liam Gallagher – most people think he's the most confident frontman they've ever seen but I know why you wear an anorak on stage: it's for comfort.

In fact, I was once so nervous about doing a central London gig at the Comedy Store on a Saturday night that I honestly contemplated getting knocked over by a car outside – just lightly enough to cause a bruise that I could show off to the manager. I thought I might still get paid that way.

Luckily *this* night was different and the nerves weren't so bad. I also knew exactly where the gig was. But as I walked and started to go over my set in my head I suddenly stopped. All of a sudden, I realized I didn't know if I needed to go left or right. I had a real panic, annoyed at myself and completely confused. I went into a newsagent and the guy drew me a map. When I saw it written down, it became obvious that I knew where I was going and I didn't need to follow it.

I walked down a very long tree-lined main road; the street lights were fairly dim and cars were speeding past. I looked ahead and noticed something walking from the gate of a house towards the road, a good seven or eight metres ahead. The little figure was briefly illuminated by the street light and then it shuffled off into the darkness towards the road. It wasn't a cat or dog or fox, it was more upright and had something white around it. White shorts?

And then…my heart stopped. I realized the white was a nappy: it was a toddler. I have never run so fast. I prayed that no cars would drive up and ran up the middle of the road into the darkness ahead. I caught sight of him, a barely one-year-old in just a nappy. I scooped him up and rocked him. I said, 'You're okay angel, let's find your mummy.' His beautiful big brown eyes looked into mine; he was as cool as a cucumber, oblivious to the fact he had just diced with death. A car zoomed past, speeding, just as I got us onto the pavement.

I could see which house he'd come from as the door was open. I walked in and shouted out; his mother froze when she saw the open door and me stood there holding her pride and joy, her heart outside of her body. I passed him over and tried to explain as best as I could.

I scanned the room. There was a baby gate on the stairs, the house seemed safe and the mother was shocked beyond belief. I've no idea how she didn't notice he'd gone but I felt she was a good parent and it had just been a terrible mistake. I left them to it. It was difficult to know what else to say.

But as I carried on walking to the gig, a strange feeling came over me. I felt very alone for the first time. A different alone feeling.

I missed him in my arms.

WHY I WANT A CHILD

Since the incident above, I've had a lot of time to reflect on how I felt that day and motherhood in general and I know for sure it's something I want. My reasoning is as follows:

 When you go for a picnic with your friends in a park I've noticed it can be quite cute if you have a little chubby toddler there too.

There used to be an advert for Fairy washing-up liquid where the little girl told her mum how soft her hands were. I want to be that mum.

 I love all the nappy adverts of babies crawling around on floors. I especially love all the white carpets and the white shirts the mums wear; basically, it all looks lush. It's brilliant that you can have a baby AND you can wear a white shirt and have a white carpet.

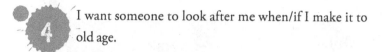 I want someone to look after me when/if I make it to old age.

I would like to have a son who likes to go shopping with me or a non-judgemental daughter who thinks I have good taste.

I absolutely love a good nativity at a primary school and I really want to stand at the back crying tears of joy because my child has just given frankincense to a baby in a manger.

I like those chubby little thighs on a baby.

I really hope my breasts grow during pregnancy and then they stay like that.

I don't want to be left out now that all my friends are having kids. I definitely don't want to be that woman who holds up her lap dog when we have a group photo on holiday.

I like going to bed early.

MAD MAM SYNDROME

I've been thinking a lot about that little baby in his nappy and working out how to have my own baby in a nappy. And the best way to make this happen is with my Jon. I mean, I know there's a 'best' way, which is also, sadly, the only way, but what I mean is I'm trying to work out how to make it seem like it's his idea. I'm essentially trying to speed it all up. He has agreed to have a child with me and has made it clear he only wants one. This is interesting, I thought. I quite like the idea of setting out to only have one. It's bit against the grain, isn't it? I like that. It's like being a fan of jazz or going to Naples on holiday – it's a bit different, it makes people go 'oh'.

I was an only child myself and I absolutely hated it* but I'm hoping my future child will enjoy it if it's got two parents at home. I'm totally fine with having one child – and that's because I think we'll end up having three.

I remember when I was 16, my mum saying to me that if I got pregnant not to worry as she would have the baby. She then corrected herself and said, 'We can share the baby.' She then corrected herself again, knowing that she didn't want to share it, to, 'I'll look after it for you but, like, all the time.'

---

* Jon – My recollection is that you told me that you also only wanted one child as you were an only child and grew up perfectly happy.

I can remember thinking, 'I bet that's what happens to women at a certain age, something kicks in and they're asking their teenage daughter to have a baby.' My mum sometimes smells my hair, still, now I'm in my thirties. I've passed it off as 'mad mam' syndrome and I know it's something that is going to happen to me too. It's not just my mum; my grandad adores babies and young children – he's been the best grandad ever. He even keeps all my baby teeth in a jar. I think I'm ga-ga about kids too, I've just got this one thing I need to deal with. I keep thinking, what if I don't like the child I have? I mean, when they're born, how can you fall in love with something you've only just met? It takes time to decide if you like someone. What if they've got bad taste in music? What if they're boring? What if they support Leeds United?

MARRIED LIFE

I have been married to 'Britain's third-favourite funnyman' Mr Jon Richardson for just under a year now. It's still early enough that my family aren't themselves around him. The other day, my uncle introduced me to his friend as 'Jon Richardson's wife', which we all found hilarious. My mum will make a naughty comment to me on the phone and instantly say, 'Don't tell Jon I said that', and my grandad wears his best shirt and stands up a lot when we go round. You really see a different side of people when they're around someone 'off telly'; the service gets better in cafés and people follow you about taking secret pictures. People seem to feel a real need to come and talk to him, take a bit of him, let him know that they know who he is – 'You're that Jon Richardson!' I want to run up and go, 'He knows who he is, dickhead!' But you can't, you have to be nice. I like that when we go to places I have to act like Meghan Markle. Jon says that I actually don't have to act like I'm married to royalty, I just have to be polite, but it's all or nothing for me.

Looking back, it really was a whirlwind romance but we were both certain almost instantly that we had met the person we'd like to journey through life with. I can't now imagine a time without him. Unless I try really hard and then it all comes flooding back: all the good times I had when I was single and carefree, all the crazy weekends…Ha!

Married life is great; though I suppose it's apt that we met at a pub called The Fighting Cocks as I'll be honest, we do argue quite a bit. I tell Jon 'it's good for us'. That's what my granny always used to say – 'If you don't argue then it means one of you is keeping their mouth shut and that's not healthy.' Also, they're not huge arguments we have, they're just the type you have in Homebase or on a car journey or when I tell one of his vegan fans that he eats meat.

LEADING A HORSE TO WATER...

To try to push Jon into having children soon, I am taking him to visit friends that have babies. I've noticed he doesn't mind sitting in the same room as a baby, so this is good. It's just that when I insist he holds the child, he gets his body into the sort of position you'd assume if you were attempting to tip over a Land Rover. It makes it all very awkward, especially if the baby is a bit of a unit.

Yesterday, we went for a walk to the chip shop and I scooped up someone's sausage dog and cradled it. The owner thought it was a bit strange but then she noticed Jon's 'off the telly'. It helped that she didn't exactly know which programme and thought his name might be Marcus. We've also just had a lovely weekend with my oldest friend, Claire, and her small toddler, Charlie. Charlie couldn't have done better if I'd paid him. He instantly struck up a bond with Jon, bordering on bizarre at times, insisting the rest of us left the room so he could smile at Jon and watch him play with his Lego.* I already know, deep in my heart, in my bones, that we will not have a well-behaved child like Charlie; we will have a child that is hard work and has very, very mad, wild hair.

But I'm yearning to argue with that child.

And I'm yearning to play the role of parent, like Claire. I just want to do all of the things she does. Like when you ask if she wants coffee and she exhales and looks you in the eye with that defeated, withered look and says, 'I really, really need a coffee, thank you.' Or when we said, 'Do you want to have a break? We'll play with Charlie,' and her whole body relaxed, her shoulders lowered, she put her head in her hands and all she could say was, '*Thank you*.' I'm looking forward to doing all that. I'm yearning to drink more wine at home between the hours of 8pm and 9.15pm, just so I can 'relax' like the mums on Facebook, and I'm looking forward to sharing memes about gin as a way of bonding with other mums.

Though I'm probably not going to be a stressed, tired mum, dependent on alcohol and crisps, stood at the bin shovelling my child's leftover chicken dippers in my mouth. I think I will still have the energy and enthusiasm to make a butternut squash soup from scratch. You see, when I think of my own imaginary child I can only picture it sleeping in a cradle and doing a little yawn. I can imagine it curled up in all those weird photo poses, like in a

---

* Jon – To be clear, the Lego was Charlie's and not mine. I suspect there will be far worse things said about me that need correction in this book but the erroneous idea that I am an adult male who plays with his own Lego in front of a toyless child does need addressing.

shoe or on a furry blanket, dressed like an acorn or a little sugar plum fairy.

The more I write, the more it's dawning on me I'm not picturing a real baby, I'm picturing a calendar. Of course, I know it's not easy having baby, I know our life will change but it's fine, I'm yearning to hold its little hand and crunch leaves underneath our matching wellies in autumn. And I'm willing to always look tired, even on the days I've slept well. That's what parenting is and I'm ready for it. I *am* ready for it, aren't I? Am I ready for it? I'm not, am I? Let's just pretend I am. As my dad said to me on the phone recently, 'Lucy, people have babies on boats.' I can manage a dry land baby, can't I?

MUMMY BIRD AND BABY BIRD

Yesterday I was feeling rather emotional. I wandered around the high street of Surbiton in posh Surrey trying to stay away from cars in case the diesel particles affected my as-yet-unconceived baby. I read about it in the *Guardian*. I felt a million miles away from friends and family in Hull. I've yet to find the soul of Surbiton.* I tried my best, though. I went and bought a couple of floaty dresses and some low heels in an attempt to fit in. I watch the women here and wonder if I'm one of them.

I'm positive that if we had a family here in Surbiton I'd feel like we were part of something, we could pop over to people's houses or something, but right now it doesn't feel like it's the right place to bring up a family.

I turned a corner and headed to Waitrose for 'some bits'. My whole life I've liked the idea of living near a Waitrose and finally my wish has come true and I feel uncomfortable about it. I know a lot of people wouldn't even understand this problem. It's because I have inherited northern working-class guilt. I think it's a good thing that I can go to Waitrose but I am also very aware I'm *in* Waitrose, if you know what I mean. I go in there and see women in headscarves and Barbour wellingtons, and men with loafers on, and I think, 'Should I really be in here?' And when I hear children saying, 'Mummy, don't forget the samphire to go with the seabass,' I recoil in horror. But then of course I'll go, 'Ooh, sushi!' and, 'Excuse me, where is your low-sugar granola?'

Yet I still feel like an outsider.

---

* Jon – There is no soul of Surbiton, that's exactly why I lived there. Surbiton, like my previous home, Swindon, is a place with houses that people live in, near some shops for them to buy food that they eat before they go to work and when they come home. Don't go looking for anything else, it's not there. There is no hidden nightclub for trendy young people who smoke liquorice roll-ups and strum their guitars when they're upset…In fact, there's nothing behind Homebase at all except some old pallets and a few hungry rats.

I passed a little wall with a bush on top of it and down by my feet, in the middle of pavement, was a tiny injured baby bird. There was no one else around. I panicked and ran back to my house. I found a little box and put cotton wool in it, ran back and scooped up the little bird. I could feel its heart beating in my hand, its chest heaving, warm. I could feel its little ribs. It reminded me of the little boy in the nappy I saved. I'm not that religious (although I do like harvest festival) but this really felt like a test, from God, from someone. I felt it happened for a reason: *I had to save this bird.*

I took it back home and called the vet in tears. The lady at the vet said they couldn't help little birds but to try the RSPB. I called the RSPB in tears and was told that there's a woman not far from us who saves pigeons. I called an Uber and kept talking to my little feathered guy; he was in a bad way. It was only the Uber driver's second-ever trip since getting his licence and he hadn't been in the country long. My Romanian is bad and his English was nearly as bad. It's hard for a northern woman to explain to a Romanian man to not go so fast over the speed bumps at the best of times but we had a real language barrier. The problem was he was a very, very chatty man and he really wanted to know what sandwiches I had in my little box and why I didn't want they to tip up. I kept saying it was a bird. I did the universal sign for bird but he kept saying, 'Ahh, chicken.' I explained I was trying to keep it alive. He was shocked and a bit scared but perhaps also didn't want to offend a possible Surbiton custom of eating live poultry sandwiches. I'll be honest with you – he was a really bad driver and the bird got knocked about a lot on that trip. I know, I know, I tried my best, I really did.

We arrived 40 minutes later at the sort of house you don't deliver an Avon catalogue to. I was a very long way from home. 'Oh,' I thought, 'I do call Surbiton home, then.'

I called the number I had been given for the pigeon lady; she said she was in Home Bargains getting cat food. I begged her to come back. I looked down at my little bird. It took a big breath and slowly faded away; its little heart stopped. It wasn't warm now. The lady on the phone said she would bury it for me. I got up, walked to the newsagents and bought a Snickers bar. I ordered an Uber home.

I can still feel the warmth of the bird's little ribcage, I can still feel the rhythm of its little heartbeat and it stopped, on my watch. For those couple of hours it was my responsibility and I failed. I'd tried my best but it wasn't enough. My day was ruined.

But now I really know I am completely ready to be a mum.

I rang my grandad on the way home in the Uber. He said you should just leave a baby bird where you found it and the mother will come back for it.

It's funny really but when I got home I felt a bit different about where I was living. In that relatively short space of time I'd had something to do, I'd had a mission. It wasn't about me or what I wanted. It felt, well, it felt like being a mum.

When it will be my turn?

GOOD NEWS

What a day!

We have just finished watching *Location, Location, Location* on Channel 4. Not only is it one of our favourite property programmes, it is by far one of our favourite programmes full stop! I don't know what it was about this particular episode, something to do with finding a bungalow with a couple of acres near Norwich or the house in Brentford that with some updating could have a lovely open-plan kitchen, but, BUT, Jon turned to me and said he will try to have a baby with me. I'm over the moon! He sort of said it like it was his idea, or at least that he has had a say in it. I remember very early in my childhood an aunt in the family telling me that the key to happy marriage with a man is making him think things are his idea. She then slapped her husband with a rolled-up newspaper for being too flat footed on her new carpet. I will never forget that day and I'm sure she'd be very proud of me.

RESULT! Look out Mothercare, here I come! (Jon won't want to come in with me – they're too hot inside and full of babies.) I instantly started looking at wall stickers for nurseries on eBay – you know, the ones that say 'Sleep well, little one' or 'You are my sunshine'. Then I thought, 'How do I want my hair on the photos when I give birth, should I go shorter? Darker?' Then I realized I had nine months to wait and I wondered if I was getting my priorities right and then for a moment, for a split second,

I panicked. Is this what we need in our lives right now? But then I felt that feeling, that feeling of holding the little bird and holding the little toddler, and how I felt when I had handed him back to his mother. Yes. This is what I want. And the nursery is going to be pale blue and I'm going to get cloud stickers and a sheepskin rug.

THE FEMALE OF THE SPECIES

I have decided I'm going to try to have a girl.

If I have a boy that's fine, I've already bought a blue 1970s retro ski jacket size 0–4 months in case I do have a boy and then I won't feel so bad about it. I've also bought some clip-on bow-ties. I've heard boys love their mothers more and if I do get a boy at least I can say 'son' a lot, which you can't do when you have a girl unless they ask you to of course and are over the age of seven. (I learn these 'woke' things on Twitter, so don't judge me.)

I read in a magazine that to have a girl you have to have sex between two-and-a-half and four days before you ovulate. I think two-and-a-half days is like in the afternoon sometime and ovulation is like when you start thinking about walking to a corner shop in the rain just to buy a Bounty bar.

I've been flirting with the idea of writing a book or large pamphlet about this phase of having a child. I might have this as my first chapter:

HOW TO HAVE A GIRL

1 You need an acid fanny.

Sorry, that's vulgar and I said to myself I wouldn't write anything vulgar but, sadly, this is what you need to have a girl. I read somewhere (disclaimer: it wasn't the *British Medical Journal*) that you need to eat acidic foods in the days leading up to ovulation. Male sperm* are less able to survive in acidic environments and eating acidic foods can actually alter the pH of your vagina. (I read this on the internet, so it's true, right?) It also did say that we should bear in mind that it's unhealthy for your body to be in an 'acidic state'.

I beg to differ. I don't know about you, but I've met a lot of older women and thought, 'Wow, you're in an acidic state.' Many of them are very healthy too, I might add. Physically, it hasn't done

---

* Jon – As opposed to…?

them any harm at all – almost as if the acidity has also killed any diseases too. Mentally, though, they are not so good, like the acid killed all the empathy. Now, thinking about this, I don't think I mean acidic, I think I mean alcoholic and that's a shame really as it is a disease. Anyway…onwards and upwards. So yep, you need an acid fanny.

2   You need to be able to count.

I've been plotting my ovulation cycle from the day of my last period until the first day of my next one. I hate the word 'period', it embarrasses me. It's taken me a long time to realize that it's not the period itself, it is the word. I'd rather the word sounded a bit more 'Hammer horror' – let's face it, you bleed, sometimes clot; it is in sync with the moon; your stomach swells; you hate yourself; everyone is a twat and if that's not weird enough, for some twisted reason in the days leading up to your period, your body makes you MORE attractive. It literally changes the structure of your face to be more symmetrical! I always remember reading an article that said Harvard University did a big research project that showed that strippers get paid more before their periods. I found this hilarious as I'm sure there are other scientific ways of finding out that females are more attractive at this time of the month. They could have just asked school children which dinner lady was prettiest.

In fact, the more I think about it, the more outrageous it is that it's called 'a period'. Here are some better suggestions:

EGG SLASHER TIME

CUTTHROAT BLOB ATTACK

THE ATTACK

ATTACK OF BLOOD

THE BRIEF WINDOW OF DEATH

THE DEATH EGG

THE CRAZE

BLOB CRAZE

RED HELL

RED HELL WEEK

DON'T YOU FUCKING LOOK AT ME, DICKHEAD

EVERYONE'S A TWAT

YEAH, YOU...TWAT

L.M.A.W.C. (LEAVE ME ALONE WITH CHOCOLATE)

Some of those are better than 'period', aren't they? I'll admit it's hard to find just one word that covers it but I think that's okay – there is, after all, a lot going on at this time of the month.

So anyway, I've been counting from my last 'attack of blood' to my next to chart my cycle so I know when we should inseminate my egg at exactly the right time to get a girl.

3 Have someone willing to inseminate you when you ask. Now, if you relate to number two in terms of personally understanding why this time needs such a horrific title, you might find it hard to find someone to inseminate you, or at least inseminate you when you ask. BUT – there are good people in this world. Strong people who can tolerate the highs and lows of womanhood and can be sensitive and supportive. You need a person like this and you need their sperm.

PART TWO

A BUN IN THE FAN OVEN

A BUN IN THE OVEN

It's Christmas and we've had a lovely time. I got a jumper from my uncle that said 'Whore, whore, whore' instead of 'Ho, Ho, Ho' (in a Hull accent it sounds the same. Underneath the writing was a picture of two half-naked women in the sleigh with Santa. I'm not sure why they're seen as whores, really – if they were men dressed like that in Lapland they'd been seen as extreme athletes). Also during the festive period, myself and 'hubby' have been wearing matching his 'n' hers elf hats. Mine has little plaits on either side so we know whose is whose.

We stayed a few days at Jon's mum's and then we went to over my auntie's house. On the way in the car, I felt really sick and dizzy, like I was going to pass out. I'd never experienced feeling so faint before. At that moment, I thought, 'Maybe I'm pregnant?' So I weed on a stick and lo and behold I was!* Jon cried, I think.

---

* Jon – Since you've already referenced us being from the north, I'd like to point out here that 'weed on a stick' is a euphemism for 'did a proper pregnancy test'. We didn't have a slash under a tree then judge whether or not Lucy was pregnant by which direction the pigeon flew after it smelled it.

He turned pale and then went 'Oh no' and then he cried.

I'm sure the series of emotions I felt were the same as everyone's. 'Oh gosh, I'm pregnant.' 'Oh gosh, I can't drink.' 'Oh gosh, it's really going to hurt.' And after all that, when I had some time alone, I did the more spiritual stuff of thinking about its furry belly, its little ribcage going in and out, its tiny beak and its broken wings.

Oh dear, I can only picture having a baby bird.

THE FIRST TRIMESTER

Well, I must say, this has been a doddle. I'm extremely lucky: no sickness, no cravings. I'm going jogging and swimming, and my skin and hair are looking fab. I must admit, the only problem is I DON'T WANT JON TO GO ANYWHERE, WHY DOES HE KEEP LEAVING ME TO GO TO SEE HIS FRIENDS, DOESN'T HE CARE ABOUT ME? WHERE IS THE HOOVER, I NEED TO CLEAN, IT'S MESSY AND DUSTY. THIS IS MY NEST, LET'S STAY TOGETHER IN THE NEST, JON, WE DON'T EVEN NEED DOORS BECAUSE WE'RE NEVER GOING TO LEAVE AGAIN. ONLY TO COLLECT TWIGS AND WE CAN DO IT TOGETHER CAN'T WE!! I'LL NESTLE ON YOUR BACK. WE CAN FLY TOGETHER.

Oh dear, I think I'm hungry. I'll just have a big plate of

heavy food. Ahh, that's better. I can think straight again. What's that you say, Jon? 'What on earth was all that about?' I was just hungry, mate. It's called pregnancy hormones. You can't cope with them? Oh this is only the beginning…

After one of these outbursts yesterday, Jon looked at me like a scared little child. 'I think your mum should come and stay for a bit,' he said.

'Okay,' I said.

Then Jon remembered what that entails.

'Can you go to the shop for me, Jon?'

'Yes, what for?' he asked.

'I really, really fancy some custard.'

MILK DUCKS

We have just attended an antenatal class and Jon has come home and practised putting a nappy on a teddy. I don't know how I feel about anything anymore. I've got rock-hard tits, I can't think straight and I really want a drink. I mean a proper drink. I even want to eat swordfish. Not because I like it or know what it looks like, just because they've banned pregnant women from eating it because of the mercury or something. That's been the first big surprise. I can't eat a fish I've never heard of – who eats swordfish anyway? – but now I really want it.

I'm finding it all a bit boring at the moment. My hormones are mental but nothing is really happening. I'm just thinking about swordfish and how I embarrassed myself at that antenatal class. The woman leading the class told us about our milk ducts and I asked why they're called 'ducks'. She said she didn't follow and I said, 'Well, ducks don't have nipples, do they?'

Now, it's maybe not right to say this but I truly believe if we were in Hull people would laugh at me and we'd move on but we weren't, we were in Surbiton. Everyone went silent – a group of adults all giving me a sympathetic look. I knew what that look meant as I'd seen it before. It was exactly the same as at university when I thought Karl Marx and Groucho Marx were brothers. Or when I once went up to someone I fancied in a band and said, 'It's like the sound isn't actually coming out of your electric guitar!' And he said 'It's not, it's coming out of the amp.'

I've always battled between being intelligent and being stupid and here I was, getting ready to be a parent and with a group of people who thought I was stupid.

'Is a swordfish actually a real thing?' I said. And then it happened, like my baby was trying to look after me. Or perhaps join in the ridicule? There was no mistaking it. I've had a few flutters in my tummy but I've not quite known what it was, but then – wallop! There it was: a proper kick. There's the baby. It's really in there?

'Shit just got real,' I thought to myself. It's got legs or/and arms, it's not some black-and-white shadows on a scan picture. This kick is important, this is timing at its best as it came just at a point where I was starting to think pregnancy was a bit uneventful. Oh boy, it's not. I've got something growing inside of me. Wow.

This is it, Miss Stupid is really having a baby.

I've started to think I'm a bit neurotic. Just a little bit. Or is that the term we use negatively to describe women who get stuff done but get upset about it? When it comes to everything in the baby department I think I might just be a bit uptight about it all. I mean, when we were trying, I charted my cycle and we both took bee pollen and some juice I'd bought off the internet to help with fertility and today I bought a special cream that you put on your – pardon for being crude – 'lady undercarriage' to help to 'stretch it' (so it hopefully won't tear, although, let's face it, it's not Play-Doh down there, is it?).

The woman who made the cream and sold it on her website is called Jan Bastard. That's her real name. I wondered if Jan knows that I, presumably like so many other mums-to-be who have bought this 'motherlylove' cream for their downstairs region, have thought of Jan while crouching down and smothering it on. It says on her website that she's retired. Some retired women make jam; not old Bastard, she makes creams at home that stretch your...you know what.

Aren't women amazing? The things we do for each other. Next time I see a Facebook post about women needing to lift each other (or stretch each other out), I'm going to mention Jan Bastard in the comments section and how thoughtful she has been to make this cream. I don't think I'm ever going to forget Jan. She's created a lasting legacy among women and their...you know whats.

THE SECOND TRIMESTER

I am now 20 weeks pregnant. We couldn't wait till the arrival; we have found out what sex our child is going to be...she is going to be a girl. But of course, if she doesn't want to be a girl she doesn't have to. I mean, great if she does but no sweat if she doesn't.

Right, wow, I'm having a girl, I'm having a girl, oh my gosh,

I'm so pleased. What am I going to do with this little boy's jacket? She can wear it anyway, with a bow in her hair. Oh no, I don't need to dress her girly, they say that's not a good thing, don't they? I'll dress her a bit of both to be on the safe side. What are we going to call her? I know what girls can be like – they're complicated but they're amazing. Right. I'm having a girl, but she shouldn't be defined by her gender. Oh gosh, do I need to get off Twitter.

No, actually, maybe I don't. They're right, this is why we're in a mess. Look at me, I can't go to the post box without eyeliner on.

I hope she isn't bitchy like me. Please don't let her be worried, comparing herself to others. Let her be a force of nature but not overbearing. Actually, she can be overbearing if she wants – when men are overbearing they're known as leaders. Oh gosh, I have read the *Guardian* too much…I'm just going to bring her up the way I was. I was given jumbo sausage rolls and little plastic heels. I had a doll that was just a head and you played with its hair and I had Barbies and I've turned out fine, sort of. I was also told not to trust men, though, and my mother warned me several times she would kill any man who touched me. My daughter will be fine: women rule the world, they just don't get equal pay.

I think it's easier for women if you don't mind never walking anywhere on your own. My mum always told me if there was someone following to just bend down and pretend to cluck like a chicken. I did once try it and I very clearly remember them saying, 'You've dropped your cashcard and your bag is open.'

Oh, a little girl! A woman! We're having a strong, independent woman, if she wants to be. Don't fuck my daughter over, I'll kill you, I'll protect her with my life. And if she wants to play with Barbies, I'll get her a screwdriver as well.

If I were having a boy I'd still have been over the moon but I really wanted a girl…Please like me, please like me.

What are going to call her? We don't agree on perineal flowers* for the garden from Homebase, we don't even agree on toilet cleaner, how are we going to agree on a name?

FOR NAME'S SAKE

Right, we had a chat about it. So I like Ivy; Jon likes Elsie, which was the name of his grandmother who passed away just before we met. I mean, I can't really argue with that, can I? He's totally got me over a barrel there so it's lucky I do really like the name. Elsie's a lovely name, it just fits. I don't know why but I just have this feeling she's going to be an Elsie. We told a few people and an aunt of mine said it was an old lady's name and under no circumstances must we call her Elsie. She was very upset about it; I haven't seen her that upset since my mother went round to her house with unshaven armpits.

'Why don't you call her a nice name, like Tania or Melanie?'

---

* Jon – Are perineal flowers something I should have learned about in the NCT class? They sound disgusting, like 'anal blossoms'.

Elsie is a great name for a little girl. Although, Jon's nanna also, by the way, hated her name, so there's a possibility she herself might not have wanted us to call the baby Elsie, although Jon's mum said she would be touched.

I will be really pissed off though if Elsie doesn't like her name either.

THE MACHINE

I'm going to give breastfeeding a really good go and not put her straight on the bottle. I've read my natural parenting book and that's what they advocate. And I read the *Guardian* and that alone means you're 21 per cent more likely to breastfeed (I made that up). I have a drama degree, so that makes it 12 per cent more likely. I have several books on yoga and a book about healing with herbs (through the roof percentage-wise, obvs). I have been to Berlin, I like wildflower meadows, I have a dish scrubber that is made of walnut kernels and I worry about plastic packaging. I'm as pro-breastfeeding as you can be apart from I haven't been to Glastonbury Festival. BUT I WILL...

To be honest, the more I read about breastfeeding, the more angry I get that it's seen as a bit of a left-field choice – the 'natural choice' rather than a 'normal choice'. I say 'normal choice' with a wince though, as I'm not comfortable even writing it. I suppose I can see both sides. On the one hand, I understand there shouldn't be a stigma around NOT breastfeeding, or any pressure. Some women decide not to even attempt it and that is their choice, but I do worry if some of that choice has been affected by mass marketing, the weight of advertising and consumerism. Hmm.

I am totally in the camp of 'fed is best'. But I've been told breast milk doesn't fill a baby up as much as formula so they wake for a feed more often. But when I researched the benefits of breast milk, it made me want to give it my best shot for as long as possible. Though my choice is based on the fact that I'm going to have support at home – it's not based just on what I feel is best for my baby, it's based on what I'm practically capable of doing for my baby. I've made a decision. I like the idea of adding a bottle of formula to a night feed but it feels weird somehow to give my baby formula made by a big commercial company with questionable morals!

Anyway, I can feel my body already preparing to provide milk. Basically, I'm like a fridge that has one of those drinks dispensers in it. I think that's the best way to describe it. I am becoming a machine. Each day, these breasts of mine, assigned at birth for this very reason, are becoming Spitfires – hard, angry, water-gun Spitfires – and I'm not afraid to use them, either of them.

(I'm hoping I can use both of them.)

The hormones have really kicked in now. Oh boy, they were there before but now they are mental. What happens is my mind starts to drift; I'll be talking about one thing and then BAM I start on another subject.

So with that in mind, here's a poem I have written about milk.

I wrote it in the break of *Location, Location, Location*. I think Kirstie and Phil may have inspired me. I really, really like Kirstie and Phil (they present a property programme on Channel 4 at the time of writing this, in case this diary is found when I'm older or dead). They help usually very middle-class couples find a house on some sort of tight budget in an area they don't really want to live in but have no choice because they still want 'period features'. I imagine the programme makers think they get their property buyers from all types of backgrounds but I have never heard anyone say they want to move house because of the drug den next door. It is basically very nice middle-class couples finding something to do with their lives and that's lovely. But there's more to this show. Much more.

There's an unspoken romance between Kirstie and Phil. At first, it seems like sisterly/brotherly mockery: she rips the piss out of him; he pretends she's bossy and then at the end they congratulate each other even if neither of them finds the couple a house. But in all of that, if your heart is open, if you can read the subtle cues, you will see that they are madly in love with each other. *Location, Location, Location* is the most epic modern romance there is.

Some people watch the show to be fooled by repeats from years ago. For example, an episode might make them think they can afford a terrace house in Brighton and they get all excited and then they realize it was filmed in 2010. But I REALLY want to know something else. It's not about property prices; in my mind it's about when did they have sex together? Because they *did* have sex together, surely? It's hidden subtext, it's definitely there.

Why else would a series carry on for 20 years?

Yes, that's right, it's been on TV for 20 years and there's one reason for that. Not semi-detached houses in Wilmslow, not bungalows on the Downs, not thatched cottages in Suffolk, not Ian and Stephanie from Coventry wanting to explore what Berkhamsted has to offer. NO. It's because it's a tale of unrequited love and unadulterated lust. It's not even a case of 'Will they? Won't they?' Oh no, for me it's '*When* did they?'

I want them to get the spotlight they deserve. I want us to march to them in droves and shout, 'Profess your love, Phil!' How many more years will the show carry on before he just says on camera, 'Fuck you, Sue, if you want an open-plan kitchen and good schools you're gonna have to cough up another 15 grand.' And then he'll get down on his knees and say to Kirstie Allsopp: 'You terrify and you complete me, you drive me wild, you are all woman and I want you right now.'

I was thinking about all this and how Phil should just *do it* when Jon turned to me and said, 'Why are you staring into space? The programme has ended.'

'I'm sorry,' I said. 'Have we got any custard left?'

Oh yeah, and here's my poem about milk:

☞ MILK ☜

We went for a country walk today,
I saw a cow in a field.
Its udders red and swollen, used, knocked about,
*   pushed and pulled*
and this was a lucky cow, not used as a milky, money-
*   making machine, pumped all day, its calf torn*
*   away,*
this was in a field, feeling the weight of its udders,
*   red and raw, like me feeling the weight of my*
*   own breastfeeding udders, the selfless act of*
*   providing.*
But I have the choice to provide.
Sad old cow, why do you taste so nice?
Why can't I be a better vegan?
You should have the right to graze all day and watch
*   your calves grow up and you should be able to*
*   pass away on a hill as the sun goes up.*
Why do you taste so nice with red wine gravy?
Why do they tell me you're good for iron, you're good
*   for my baby.*
And then tell me your cooked flesh causes cancer?
I think I've found the answer.

I'll think about the taste of freedom when I get that
      craving,
I'll think about the drops of milk on your little baby
      calf's tongue,
and be more human,
be a hero,
be unsung.

HYPNO-MUM

My mum rang me. I told her last week that I was thinking about doing hypno-birthing and that I'd booked to see someone who teaches it. It's like hypnotism but I don't think you go into a trance. It helps with relaxation and studies have shown it can have really positive outcomes. I'm into all this sort of stuff. I believe in the power of healing and meditation.

'Lu, I've bought this brilliant hypno-birthing CD,' my mum said excitedly.

'Oh great,' I said. 'Thanks for that.'

My mum paused. 'Yeah, it really helps me fall asleep. I wouldn't be without it now; you should get one.'

We went for the private hypno-birthing class with a lovely lady called Louise at her home in a converted church. She's had four kids and her house was covered in pictures of rabbits.

After the initial embarrassment of recognizing Jon but making him wait in the entrance hall while she tried to remember the name of the show he was on, we then got cracking. She asked me why I was hesitant about giving birth. I explained in detail, with the actions, all the horror stories I'd heard and then she did something I wasn't expecting. She asked Jon to stand up. I thought, 'Oh gosh, what's she going to do with him? It's not Jon's fault that historically women have suffered in childbirth.'

Louise told us that she would first practise the hypno-birthing on Jon as he will be the one to help me with it when I'm in labour. I would have paid three times the fee if I'd known she was going to ridicule him this much. She tried to teach him how to speak softly and we all started laughing as he could only sound creepy; then she tried to get him to relax – again, something he's not capable of doing. She taught him some of the speech to say to me.

'You are calm, you are walking in a garden, you see a magic carpet, you get on it…' She asked him to whisper it to me. But when Jon said it, he sounded like he'd abducted me.

It was then my turn and I reacted well to it. Louise said that I found it easy to relax. I explained I can ramp up from 0 to 60 very quickly. Jon nodded. 'But I can also calm down quickly,' I said. 'I think it's because I napped a lot as a child.'

We were then instructed to never use the word pain when taking about childbirth and to always say 'surges'.

I looked Louise in the eye and said, 'Is it going to hurt?'

She sighed and took off her glasses. 'No, Lucy, not if you

master the breathing techniques on CD five.'

'Where's CD five?' I asked. 'I've only got three here.'

'That's available on my website. I accept PayPal now.'

I walked out of there feeling confident, calm and in control.

Jon thought I might need a little holiday. Weird, not sure why. He actually said, 'I think you might need a little holiday,' in the same tone as someone says, 'I think you should put the knife down.' I was eating a crumpet at the time and unwrapping a picture my grandad had done for Elsie's playroom. Without causing any offence, the picture is very mystical. It's a copy of a very famous French painting of a little pixie-type woman with long legs and flowing hair in a sort of woodland at night, slightly bewitched. The sky is red. I'll be truthful, she's got mad eyes, but I adore my grandad and there's none better with kids than him – he's got the gift – and if he thinks it should be in a child's nursery then it will be! Until we can replace it with a poster of Peter Rabbit.

We decided to have a few days in Cornwall and I couldn't be happier. I hardly ever get to go down to Cornwall, it's just too far away, but I was born in Truro so it feels like the motherland. I have this fantasy that at some point they'll stop letting people who aren't Cornish buy in Cornwall. I know that won't really happen but I wish it would. I love the idea that I could flash my birth certificate and be given some sort of Cornish birthright. Or if someone said to me in a back-end pub, 'You're not from here,' I could whip out my birth certificate. Though the remarkable thing in this scenario would be me being able to locate my birth certificate. However, I should just point out that we weren't living in Cornwall when I was born, they had me on holiday. I must tell you that story one day.

The car journey to Cornwall was beautiful. As you head west, you watch the greens turn greener, the soil get softer and people's complexions get rosier. Cornwall really feels like a different country. It's a spiritual place and I can honestly say this was the most spiritual time Jon and I have had. You see, Jon's not a spiritual man. He's a realist. He's a humanist but he's scientific, he's practical. He can't cope with disappointment, he doesn't believe in an afterlife, in 'energy', in mediumship, sixth senses, healing, crystals or aliens. I'm so far and away the other way. When I go to a hotel reception I say to the person behind the desk when they hand me my key, 'Has anyone died this room?' If they're not sure, when I go up I'll get a feeling as to whether anyone has and, as a result, I might find I need to upgrade to a bigger room.

And look at my mum. She had something in her ear for years. I took her to the best ear doctor on Harley Street but he couldn't help. He said that never in 35 years had he not been able to remove impacted ear wax. So what does that tell you? Yes, that's correct – it was an alien chip. Me and my mum have always known that aliens are around us – we've seen things, felt things. We once saw a big orb of bright fluid float up past the window. My mum did kung fu at it; I've never seen reaction speeds like it. I managed to talk to Professor Brian Cox about it when I worked on his radio show. I asked what it could have been and he said, 'I think it was a balloon.' I was rather disappointed with that. Anyway, this thing in my mum's ear, eventually it fell out on her carpet, making a 'heavy' sound like metal and then the cat ate it. The cat then disappeared for days. Spooky.*

During our drive into Cornwall, we both needed a wee (not sure I needed to mention that). Jon said there were lots of junctions coming up with roads that went into little villages. We couldn't decide which one to turn off at but rather than look up a country pub we thought we would let fate decide. This isn't something Jon would usually say or agree to but we were both so relaxed. I said, right, let's turn in two junctions time, so we did. We drove through a pretty little village trusting we'd find a pub and oh boy, did we find one. We found a pub that was in the shape of an old shoe, next to a thatched pub, which is one of the oldest pubs in the country. We just sort of looked at each other and said, 'This is the one.'

Jon said that he had a tingle down his spine but didn't know why. I already knew before we stepped into the pub that

---

* Jon – Reading this paragraph, I think I now need a holiday.

something was special, that this day would be a day I'd remember for a very long time.

I looked at Jon. 'We've been led here, haven't we?' I asked him.

Jon looked back at me and said, 'Yes, we have.'*

We walked into the pub and I have never seen anything so bizarre and wonderful. It was dark and dusty, like a hobbit pub, and full of strange artefacts. It felt like we were stepping into another world. I told the woman behind the bar I had a Cornish birth certificate. She nodded and asked if we wanted straws with our drinks. I think she sensed we were from the artistic community.

Jon sat down and I went to the toilet. In the corridor next to the toilet was the exact same French picture my grandad had replicated for Elsie's bedroom! I rushed back to tell Jon. He told me to listen. A little blonde-haired girl had just arrived with her parents – she was called Elsie. I began to tear up. I really felt I was getting a message from my granny who passed away or from my ancestors or from someone to say they knew I was having a baby, like a blessing. The mind is a wondrous thing, isn't it? It can play tricks on us. But as Noël Coward said, 'There are more things in Heaven and earth than are dreamt of in your philosophy.'

When we were ready to leave, we had a look at another room in the pub along a narrow corridor. There was a big old wooden door that looked like it once belonged to a ship. I went to open it

---

* Jon – Although I am still laughing having read it, I have to confess I have no recollection of this 'Mulder and Scully'-style exchange. I suspect I might have been referring to the satnav when I agreed that we had been guided there by something greater than both of us.

to have a look in the next room but I got such an overwhelming feeling that I couldn't do it.

'That door…' I said to Jon, 'I can't shake off how I feel when I just touched that door.'

We sat in the car in silence. Jon couldn't believe how he felt, truly believing we were meant to have gone there – a feeling he'd never had before.

'That door,' I said again.

I couldn't let it go so I called my grandad. He said he was in the middle of tracing his family tree and had made a discovery: he knew his family had always been trawlermen in Hull but he'd now been able to trace that they went right back to the days of whaling – it turns out we belong to some of the first families that lived and worked in that area. I told him about the pub and he thought that it was lovely – he said to see it all as a blessing.

I googled the history of the pub and found out, are you ready for this? The door came from a Hull whaling boat!

There is of course no way to know if this boat had held ancestors of mine, other than the intense feeling I had when I touched it! We came back after our few days away rosy cheeked and full of happiness and joy. I was ready to have my baby; my ancestors had blessed me. I was sure of it.*

---

* Jon – For all my cynicism, I have to confess that this was a very memorable day. To have found, AT RANDOM, a pub in the middle of nowhere that did vegan pie, chips and gravy and served what is, to this day, one of the best pints of Dark Mild (which you can't find bloody anywhere these days) I've had in my life, was remarkable. And it wasn't raining.

TITS

I have bought another illustrated book about 'natural parenting' and there are lots of swirly pictures that end up looking like tits and a lot of naked women howling at the moon.

Tonight we attended a breastfeeding class. I tried not to look at any of the other couples. Some of them were too European to recognize Jon but his face was familiar to them and I was embarrassed. I just didn't want them to know I had breasts. The older lady running the class was very eager to point out that she does not get paid for the lessons and all the proceeds go to charity – she just very much wanted to pass on the wisdom and craft of natural feeding. She was a type of woman I have seen in village halls up and down the country, usually in yoga poses, sometimes trying to save trees, sometimes in *Annie Get Your Gun* trying to sing in tune at the back of the chorus. The lady had brought a doll that we passed around to practise our feeding positions. It turns out you don't actually put the baby to the nipple; you make the baby stretch its head, tickle their nose with your nipple until they try to bite it out of anger and just as their little mouth is at the widest angle, like a crocodile, you shove the nipple in and away they go.

Two things I found bizarre about this class:

1 She made the men practise the breastfeeding position, the same as the women. (Just to be clear, she didn't make the men pretend to get breast milk from the women – she basically treated the men like they were mothers; they all had to pretend with the doll, to the point where the men were almost upset when they realized at the end that they couldn't do it in real life!)

2 The lady had rather ample-sized breasts. Nothing extreme, just, if I'm to say, a nice pair of tits – very firm and lifted I thought, for her age. Now the only reason I noticed it – and everyone in the room noticed – is she used her own breasts to demonstrate with. When she wanted to show us how to express milk, she squeezed and squeezed them. When she explained latching on, she yanked and shoved them. She slapped one about a bit, stroked them, pinched them…it became more and more bizarre to the point where, towards the end, there was sort of an unsaid thought from all of us: has this woman only decided to run these lessons because she likes playing with her titties?

We need to buy a pram.

'Fine,' said Jon, 'Let's go.' He said it too confidently, too nonchalantly, so I knew he didn't understand.

'You don't understand, we need a Bugaboo pram.'

It meant nothing to him and yet my every waking thought was consumed with this essential designer item needed from birth. I showed him the Australian advert for it on YouTube: a tall, slim, boring couple with the beautiful dream pram on a beach.

'We don't live near a beach,' he said.

'It doesn't matter,' I replied. 'It's the colour palette, it's unique.'

Jon then asked to see the price. You can't water down £869. He looked at me with his *Question Time* face. 'No way.'

I fell to the floor. 'IT'S MORE THAN JUST A PRAM, IT'S GOT A FOOTMUFF,' I wept. For a moment the sadness cut so deep that I wondered if the real reason I had wanted to be impregnated was just so I could have a Bugaboo. 'I think I'll love our baby more if I have one. The pram colour is beige, Jon.'

None of this was working.

'It's your hormones, Lucy,' he said. 'I think.'

It wasn't my hormones, it wasn't...

Except it is. You see, I know I've got them raging away but I can't stop myself.

I'm buying maternity clothes from an online eastern European website that agrees with me that pregnant women should dress provocatively. I just can't find anything in Next with an extending belly band that shows off cleavage AND leg. I don't really understand why, in my most contemplative, feminine nesting period I want to look like a slut. I mean, I do understand a bit. I've never had breasts as big and firm as this and no one wants to touch them, I've asked everyone.

'You don't want a designer pram. You're not a snob,' said Jon.

Now this hurt, this hurt a lot. I AM a snob, you see. For me, in the headspace I'm in, he's basically saying 'Your legs weren't long enough to go horse riding like the other girls even if your single mother could afford it' and 'You'll never live in a Farrow & Ball country cottage with Hunter wellies and an Aga and a dog called Stephanie'. But that's what I want, eventually – I want to be in one of those interior design magazines that no one buys. I still want to be working class when it suits me, though. I don't want to be put in a box. I don't even like the two terms. Surely there's a better way to define the two classes? Could it be the 'shared bathwater' class versus the 'been to Center Parcs twice' class? I'm proud to say I'm both.

This pram thing has thrown up a few tricky issues. I want to live in London but I want my child to have a northern accent and

I want it to have the best bits of being middle class and the best bits of being working class. I know I'm both because before I was up the duff I went to Sainsbury's for an organic Malbec as we were having Italian and on the way out I tripped up and I took the impact with my face and saved the wine.

Another way I know I'm both is because when I moved to Jon's house in Surbiton, my main goal in life was to be accepted in Waitrose – which I now have been. I'd spent most of my adult life until this point with not much money and although it's hard for everyone in that predicament it is especially hard when you are trying to make people think you go skiing in France. I may live in a semi in Surrey now but I know there are still some things that mark me as different to the women around here, and one of those things is I've only just found out who John Lewis is. We didn't have John Lewis in Hull. I do believe if you are connected to a John Lewis it will add several years to your life expectancy. Now, when I go to our local John Lewis it feels like the very essence of being a middle-class mother. It's like the earthenware is hugging me. I feel safe, I feel at one, I have arrived.

There are customers in that shop who have always bought their towels from John Lewis. In Hull, we get our towels from Tony's Textiles, yet when I walk around John Lewis, after a while, I get very homesick. Maybe it's because I'd love Hull to have had a John Lewis. The nearest thing was Hammonds. I think everyone remembers that posh shop in town that you wore your best coat to and your mum would brush 'bits' off it before you left. The high street is collapsing but people will always want places to dress up for.

Anyway… A big eye opener to which class I'm in was when we designed our kitchen together. Jon and I argued about the fridge. I said we need to put it behind a cupboard door out of sight, as that's what they do 'round here. 'We haven't worked in comedy for all these years, Jon, to be able to see our fridge!' He gave in but because I'm working class, I missed fridge magnets. We still love getting them as gifts but we have to stick them to the side of the kitchen scales. They're still well hidden, though. I tested to make sure you can't see them when you walk in. There's one with a cartoon of two pigs having sex in Lanzarote and I like that. I have not forgotten my roots!*

I've got friends who have done well for themselves and they've got no handles or cupboard knobs. They're too posh to open their kitchen doors – you just sort of lightly push. It's confusing at first but that's the intention. It makes them feel superior. Their relatives come over and say, 'Ooh, I don't know how to open this,' and they reply arrogantly, 'No, that's right, you don't.'

One of my friends hid her bin in a cupboard and her auntie said, 'Ooh Kathleen, I can't find it anywhere!' And Kathleen said, 'No, well, you should have worked harder in school, then.' Savage.

There's an update on the pram situation. We have just bought the cheapest pram in Mothercare. Jon was right – it steers well, it is

---

* Jon – It is not two pigs having sex, I wouldn't have bought that. It is one pig having numerous sexual experiences with two human women. Everybody involved looks to be having a lovely time, before anyone writes in.

light and easy to fold up. But alas, there's no magic to it. I know I'll be an outcast with the other Surbiton mums but, equally, I know I'm wearing a maternity mini-skirt and you can practically see what I had for lunch.

I'm being silly. I know I am. Me and Jon are from humble beginnings; no one in our inner circle is showy and, after all, I want the baby to be grounded. Yes, she will enjoy avocados but I will take her to greasy spoon cafés and not wipe the gravy off her chin all day, and I'll let old ladies swoon over her and put a shiny coin in her hand, and we'll go on dodgy caravan holidays and eat potato waffles and that will be a very good childhood indeed.

But I'm telling you now, that bright red pram in the hallway – I'm going to fucking run it to the ground before the baby arrives and then I'm going to get a Bugaboo off eBay.

I'VE STILL GOT A LOT OF HORMONES

I don't know what's wrong with me, I keep feeling sad and happy and emotional. I saw a little girl today in the park who looked just me when I was her age and it made me think about our baby girl.

I had a bit of puppy fat growing up – skinny little legs and bit of a belly – but, unsurprisingly, when I stopped putting a whole Sara Lee gateau in the microwave, pouring it into a mug and drinking it, it went away. I was never sporty and the little girl I saw in the park didn't seem sporty either, and nor did her mum. She looked like she makes a good cold buffet, and that's a good thing. The mum was helping her daughter to play tennis – well, I say this, but she was actually just trying to help her hit a ball with a bat and sadly she'd try to show her how to do it and then miss as well.

I cried. First I gave her a sympathetic look like the one people give me, then I felt bad and then I cried for them both. I knew what had happened here – that mother didn't belong in a park trying to hit a ball, she needed to be in a hot tub drinking prosecco with her mates. I knew that the little girl must be anxious about PE.

I bet she's been picked on for being shit as she was really bad at hitting a ball and probably worse at catching one. I was too. I will never forget the sound of 30 children shouting at you to catch a ball when you're playing rounders on the school field. Awful. I can still feel the dread of a PE day, the anxiousness of it – having to undress next to other girls, going out onto a freezing cold field in front of boys and exposing how crap I was, particularly at running. My mum said I didn't have the legs for running. Nothing about PE showed off my best points. My small bandy legs and arms. What I do know is that I'm a bloody fast runner if a dog is chasing me, like that one after I did a double shift at Asda. You can't really set dogs on children to help them run faster but it wouldn't surprise me if some of those pro-tennis mums you hear about have tried it as a warm-up.

As I got a bit older, I'm pretty sure I learned to smoke with the older girls just so I could skip PE. The only thing I was good at in this subject was putting the mats away.

I just never want this beautiful baby to feel like that and if she does then I will always fake notes for her. What I liked doing as my exercise when I was a kid was going on a long walk and singing my head off and sitting somewhere for a nice picnic. Why can't that be a lesson? Yep, I'll write every excuse note under the sun for my baby if there's one shred of insecurity at school.

Oh, look at me, getting upset about things that haven't happened! And that's just one example.

My hormones really are MENTAL. I knew about 'nesting mode' but I thought I'd just be on my hands and knees dusting the skirting boards. But I can't bend down, I'm massive. I love being massive, I love my bump, but I've seen her on the scan and she's tiny so I don't know why there's so much padding. I hope she doesn't expect this much comfort on the outside world; it will cost a fortune in duck down and feather pillows and, as we know, shag-pile carpets are very out of fashion.

I didn't know the nesting hormones would mean I wanted to mother everything I saw. I saw this on Facebook:

> *Looking to rehome a pet bull, not for sale but for safe keeping. We're no longer able to keep him where he currently is and if not gone by Wednesday he'll be sold to the slaughter which we're desperately trying to avoid at all costs. He's a short-horned cross limousine, dehorned, castrated, well humanized and very friendly named Bullby and we will pay for his expenses. If anybody has any ideas where we could keep him it would be highly appreciated.*

I started to think about the back room. It used to be the garage and surely we can get some hay in there for baby bulls? I just really want to bring the bull home and cuddle him and take him to Alton Towers and the seaside and let him have parties with his little bull friends.

Gosh, I need to give birth to this baby soon.

CRY BABY

I'm STILL so, SO emotional, everything is making me cry. I laughed at my best mate Jackie when she was pregnant for crying big, almost cartoon tears at an advert where someone lost a very long scarf. Now look at me, I'm a mess. Anything will set me off. We went to a bakery to get some lunch and there were gingerbread men and one of them had his head knocked off. It was on a slant and although he still had a happy smile like the other one I could tell he was in distress. It made me cry and I wanted to scoop him up and rock him but I didn't want to pay £1.20.

We left the shop after the staff started to give me mucky looks – I think I'd put greasy fingerprints on the glass counter. When you're having as much butter in coffee as I'm doing that tends to happen. I'm having a lot of butter because it's in a book I'm reading that says you're allowed to do that. I'm basically eating what I want, when I want, apart from swordfish.

I'm approaching my due date fast!

Surprisingly, it seems the baby quite likes being in a warm, safe place and getting fed steak. I must add that the steak is sometimes vegan and sometimes just cow, it really depends on what article I've last read about how it does/doesn't give you cancer. I also think the baby particularly wants to stick around for the coconut smoothies. I blend a tin of coconut cream and a mushy banana and sometimes a chocolate Penguin bar. Mix them all together – coconut smoothie! I once read that it's an ancient eastern custom to give bananas to pregnant women. I can only imagine this ancient custom was at a time before we could also get a multi-pack of Penguins for £2 from Iceland. The thing is, I don't even think any of these things is why I've put on over three stone. I don't even think it is the butter in the coffee – I think it's when I started drinking custard.

I've decided that drinking custard is quite symbolic, really. For me, it's both unshackling myself from the societal pressure of what women should drink – the fad diets, Gwyneth Paltrow with her coconut water, the gin and tonic craze, the clever marketing ploys of making bottled water a luxury item – and it's also about reconnecting with my childhood, the very essence of growing up in a warm-hearted, working-class city where custard is love. And not just custard – Tip Top too, which is like basically the milk they had in the war but rebranded, and Miracle Whip, which is basically whipping cream for state schools. I'm sat here with a pint of custard saying NO to your water and fizzy drinks – they're not thick enough – and NO to your smoothies and your 'thick shakes' – they're not yellow enough. Drinking custard is a feminist revolt, it's anti-establishment. For too long they've told me what I should drink.

Oh my gosh, I'm leaking. I mean, my 'you know whats' are leaking…MILK. I'm leaking breast milk. I'm so sorry it's a bit disgusting but…oh my god, it's yellow, the milk is slightly yellow. I've changed my milk INTO CUSTARD. I'm LEAKING CUSTARD, FUCKING HELL!

So I spoke to my midwife, Claire. I like Claire; she's got spunk. I want to ask her to be my mate but she's a bit younger than me and she blushes when Jon walks in the room. He's already signed a mug for her sister's boyfriend.

LUCY:
> *Claire, it's me, Lucy, I need to tell you I've been consuming more than an average amount of custard and then what happened was yellow milk came pouring out of me.*

CLAIRE:
> *Breast milk?*

LUCY:
> *Yes, Claire.*

CLAIRE:
> *That's normal.*

LUCY:

It was yellow.

CLAIRE:

Yeah, that's okay.

LUCY:

Have I turned it into custard?

CLAIRE:

Yeah, sort of. Your breast milk is made up of fat and water so the more fat you have the more it will add it to your milk. It also tastes of what you've eaten. Breast milk can go a bit spicy too, so it's important to have a range of food to encourage a varied diet in your baby. Or that's what they say; I just gave mine formula. Watch out for onions.

LUCY:

In what way should I watch out for onions?

CLAIRE:

Can make baby gassy.

LUCY:

Thanks Claire, I think I need to digest all that.

CLAIRE:

The custard?

LUCY:

Yeah. No, the onions. Cheers.

Spunky, you see. She's a great midwife. I'll be sad when I don't have appointments with her any more.

THE MEXICAN

We are really enjoying a thing called Deliveroo. It's a fairly new thing aimed at people who have been to Center Parcs and only drink in quiet pubs – snobs, really – who want a takeaway but don't want the local Chinese because it's too salty. Instead you get something that would be restaurant quality if it wasn't microwaved, put in a bag and biked over to you. I LOVE IT.

Tonight we got burritos. The burrito I ate was really heavy but because it was all rolled up like it was used to smuggle cocaine I didn't realize how much food it actually was. I devoured it and for a moment I enjoyed the fullness in my tummy. It got to bedtime and I was suddenly quite tight around my chest and then I couldn't catch my breath. I kept saying to Jon, 'I can't breathe.' He rang triage at the hospital and they told us to drive over. Jon was so pale, he looked like he was going to faint as he rushed to get the car unlocked. On my way out, I noticed a little jar of mint humbugs and just placed two in my mouth at either side in my cheeks. Now, I don't know what you think but I calmed down slightly when I realized I fancied a little boiled sweet. I've watched lots of *Casualty* on TV and they never ever say, 'My heart! Pass us a mint before I go, love.'

Jon did a double take. He looked at me, distraught. 'Lucy?' he said. 'Your lips are swollen up!'

'No, don't worry, it's just a mint.'

Jon was so relieved, then ten minutes later it dawned on him too that no one rushes off to the hospital in an emergency and sucks on confectionery.

In the hospital I had an initial check-up and I had to walk up and down the hall as they kept an eye on my heart rate. I felt very looked after. But while I was walking down the long corridors something shifted in me. I burped. I burped so loudly that Jon heard it as he nervously sat in the hospital room. It was about 1am in the morning at this point and although the staff were very attentive they kept asking us to wait until a consultant had finished all the real emergencies and could sign me off. This was also because they wanted to make us pay for wasting their time, or so I thought at the time. I went back into the hospital room. Jon had tilted his cap over his face and had his eyes closed. I went to explain to him but he got there first.

'It's that fucking burrito you ate,' he said.

'It might be, it's best to get checked out.'

'We've been awake half the night because you had indigestion.'

'It could well be that, Jon, but we don't know.'

I burped again.

'Nice to see the hospital we'll be coming to,' I said, trying to blow the burrito smell away. We'd decided recently that we were going to have a waterbirth but we'd be having it here.

Eventually the consultant arrived. I told her I had eaten a burrito that was the weight of my head; she explained to me that the baby had pushed my tummy upwards and they were both fighting for room.

It was a long, quiet journey home.

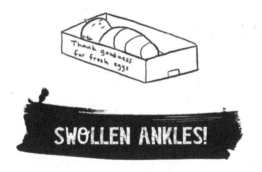

Thank goodness for fresh eggs

SWOLLEN ANKLES!

I'm hot and uncomfortable.

I feel like I should write something more interesting at such a special time in my life. Maybe I should also touch on the political landscape right now, but I'm not Dickens, am I, and quite frankly he didn't have swollen ankles.

I feel like I've picked a fight with my own comment there. Well, I have. I could pick a fight with anyone at the moment. I think this is biological, though. I don't think if we lived in the wild anyone would pick a fight with me today. I can't run very fast, I can only waddle, but I could chin someone if they crossed me. This sounds very violent, doesn't it? Well, I'm protecting my baby. The instincts are there but the sabre-toothed tiger has been replaced by the vacuum cleaner I stubbed my toe on.

I don't need the fight-or-flight reactions but they're still there and they come out at trivial things at the moment. This morning, I noticed the TV remote is sticky because I got a bit of custard on it and it got me so angry and then it made me tired and then it made me hungry and then it made me sleepy and then I woke up from a nap feeling happy and blessed and then I got hungry and then of course I got angry and this has carried on in a loop. This is classic third trimester and you don't mess with a woman in her third trimester – she is turning into a warrior. An angry, hungry, sleepy, weepy WARRIOR.

We're going to have a picnic in Richmond Park today. I think deep down I'm hoping if I eat my body weight in vegan sausage rolls the baby will pop out. I'm struggling to know if a veggie diet or a meat-eating diet is best for the baby. Yesterday I had a steak, today I had a hummus sandwich.

They say to eat the rainbow of colours, which is good because I'm also adding pastel colours to that, with a lot of pink wafers and those little Love Heart sweets. Food seems the only pleasure at the moment – in the material world, at least. In the spiritual world and in my body I'm full of love and wonder for the little baby bird I'm growing in my tummy; we are connected, we are one and I don't want it to end. I like her in my belly as I can't forget her, meal times are easy, she doesn't need playdates – none of those jungle soft-play places – and I don't need to put her to bed. Why can't they just stay inside? I'm also worried that the beak and wings will hurt when I give birth.

I've cleaned the tray in the fridge that we keep the veg in, scraping away those tiny bits of green spinach leaves that get stuck. I've dealt with all the little bits of stuff that if you have a life you leave – those little marks left by the condiments, that little sticky patch that when you're busy, busy, busy you just forget about. I've got nothing else to do, really. I don't feel important to anyone, I'm just a machine today, that's how it feels. I'm trying to pretend I'm not anxious but I am.

Jackie, my dear, dear best friend, told me that the first poo after her baby was born was nearly as bad as childbirth due to all the haemorrhoids. My mum has told me at least once a month for the last 34 years about the piles I gave her. It was so bad she had to sleep on a rubber dinghy. I've been thinking a lot about when I was born myself, the bits of bizarre information I've been given about it. I've asked all of the people present and they all relate the same story. This is how it went:

My dad was busy working away and didn't know my mum, my grandad, my granny and my auntie Rachel had all decided to go on a camping trip to Cornwall. (And oh yeah, the marriage didn't last very long, sadly!) My mum had been to the doctors and said she'd like to go on a caravan holiday and he said, 'Well, you've got six weeks until your due date so go for it, lass.' So off she went for a lovely sunny week in Cornwall. You can guess what happened next.

The legend goes that mum's waters broke while sleeping next to her sister on a caravan site in Truro. That night, my granny had got so drunk at the club house she'd slept in her boots, which was lucky because she'd needed them when they rushed my mum to the nearest hospital in the early hours of the morning. Mum said she had a fit and nearly swallowed her tongue and when I was delivered I had jaundice. Although my mum asked the doctors if I had a suntan because she did! She then looked out of the window and saw bunnies hopping. Her sister, my auntie Rachel, doesn't think that part is true, due mainly to the fact there wasn't a window.

My dad arrived and was annoyed they'd taken her on holiday. (How did he not know?) My grandad and dad then had an altercation in the corridor. (This is totally normal and actually quite a bonding experience if you live in Liverpool or you're from the north east.) I think my dad then went back to wherever he was and my mum and granny and grandad and aunt then went back to Hull. They had nothing to bring me home in but my granny went to a fruit and veg shop and inside was a wooden crate in the shape of a cradle and it said 'Thank goodness for fresh eggs' on it. She asked if she could have it, lined it with fabric and I slept in it all the way home to my grandparents' – where I presume we lived for a bit until my mum and dad were reunited and rented a flat above a dry cleaners.

Oh, and this is the bit that has scarred me the most: my grandad had always had a beard for as long as anyone could remember. But when he walked into the hospital his wife and daughter didn't recognize him because he'd shaved it off. I asked my grandad why he did this and he said it was so when it grew back it would be the same age as me! He wanted his facial hair to be like a weird hairy twin for me.

So…I wonder what *my* baby's birth will be like?

I mean, I can't top my own birth, can I, and I don't think I want to! I want my baby's birth to be painless and quick. I want Jon to look at me and tell me I'm amazing. I want to have a beautiful waterbirth and I want the midwife to say, 'Wow, we've been telling women for years that you need big hips for child bearing but your cervix is like elastic!' I want us to be bashful about the fact it only took me 12 seconds from start to finish and that the baby came out in one of those sacks – it wasn't even attached to an umbilical cord as it had already sorted that out itself inside, a bit like how some people are just good at winding up cabling. I want there to be no blood and for the doctor to say, 'Would you like us to find you a bit of blood, just so you don't feel short changed?'

I'd like my hair to look shiny and flowing and for me to look so radiant in the post-birth pictures that I don't feel I can put them on Facebook in case they intimidate other mothers-to-be. I'd like the baby to just curl up on my chest and just stay there, sleeping, stuck to me securely like Velcro.

Straight after getting back from the hospital, I'd like to go for a little run and come back and look in the mirror and think, 'Wow, I look better an hour after childbirth than I did when we had a week away in Majorca, my tummy is so flat!' Yes, I'd like the baby to give me a tan and I'd like her to wake up from her little naps within office hours.

I have manifested it thus and opened it up to the universe, just like how Noel Edmonds does.

It will happen!

PART THREE

OUT SHE COMES AND AWAY WE GO

THE BIRTH

Anyway…

Last week I went into labour. I was in labour for 26 hours.

It was all going so well before, wasn't it? I was loving my huge belly, loving the chilling and the nesting and even the fat ankles that appeared overnight. Then things changed. She was two days late, then four, then eleven, then we started with those weird things they say you should do – you know, adding chilli sauce to the butter in the coffee – and then the pineapple chunks came out and anything else someone once lied about 400 years ago. Everyone wanted my baby to pop out – except me and my baby. We were happy as we were.

But then I started having weird dreams. I had one dream in which I put my hand 'up there' and tried to break whatever they break to get things moving. The next day, we had to visit the midwife and she put her hand up there. It was a shame she did that, as we'd been getting on so well up to this point. I was going to invite her to a coffee morning and thought maybe we'd set up a WhatsApp group for a few months. But she severed the relationship after she put her whole hand up my… And then, can you believe, another nurse did it the next day. I started to feel like I was the human equivalent of a lucky dip bucket.

After much waiting, finally it happened. My waters broke in my sleep. It wasn't so much a gush, it was more like the little wee you do in primary school on a trip to learn about the Tudors (weird, I don't know where that came from).

Anyway, I woke Jon up and basically what he did was acknowledge the piss running down my leg and very matter-of-factly went into his office and, no word of a lie, he switched on his computer and he bought A FOUR-MAN TENT. I have asked the question, 'What are you doing?' many, many thousands of times in my life I'm sure, but this time it was like I really deeply understood the meaning of the words: 'What on *earth* are you doing?'

He replied, 'There's usually a long wait now, just getting some essentials.'

We went to the hospital triage like they told us to, just to check things over, and then the plan was to go home again, to relax into it, get our things and, only once I was almost fully dilated, come back to the hospital and have the baby. It felt so peaceful in there as we strolled down a corridor with all the windows open to show the nurse the wee on my sanitary towel. There was such a stillness to this summer's night as the warm, polluted Surrey air mixed with the smell of Dettol and several years of underfunding.

This is where we started to deviate from the plan. The nurse told us very apologetically but in no uncertain terms that I

MUST NOT go home and progress on my own as there was meconium (baby poo) in the waters and that could mean the baby is distressed. We had to stay at the hospital.

All my birth stuff was at home! No incense sticks and soul music.

Please tell me I could I still go in the birthing pool? No. Things had changed, they told me.

Before tonight, I'd had the feeling that anything was possible. Now I began to feel that THE MAN – i.e., doctors, Bill Gates, Richard Branson, the Dyson bloke – was interfering with MOTHER nature! If you've seen that advert from the nineties for deodorant where the woman is actually a tree and peels herself away from it then you'll know the exact image I have in my mind when I say mother nature.

The thing is, I KNOW MY BODY. Well, I really did feel I knew my body and I knew my baby and we had a connection.

In that moment, at the hospital in the dead of night, the one and only thing I felt sure of was that my baby was not in distress. As the new age books had told me, a baby can also just poo because it was now of an age when these things started to happen.

'She's not in distress, Jon,' I told him. But it was sort of irrelevant – the science was there and the science saves lives and they were already preparing me a room and finding a spare monitor as the baby would have to be monitored at all times, which meant I would have to be attached to a machine. None of this, the books told me, would help with the 'relaxation'.

I wondered in that moment whether, if I'd put my foot down

and opted for a home birth, the baby wouldn't have been late – if the lateness was to do with feeling anxious about coming into the hospital or even just going against my better judgement. The books I'd read really empowered a woman to think of birthing as a personal and precious act that *you* control and, well, I hadn't taken that route. I'd considered what Jon wanted me to do too and he felt it was safer if we did a water birth at the hospital. I know some people might say that it should be up to me what I want but Jon has a full driving licence, a mortgage and has never been in debt. I do have a degree and he quit his, so I am harder working, I'm just not sensible. In all seriousness, I wouldn't be able to relax if he wasn't fully relaxed so I trusted him, I trusted us as a unit.

But even so, it was a real punch in the guts not being able to go home and progress naturally, and something about the 'distressed' part gutted me. I'd done everything I could do to make my womb a nirvana for my baby girl. I'd done all the yoga poses on YouTube; I'd slept and laid so that she'd never tilt back – symbolic of my love really: I will prop you up all your life. So to have someone tell me my baby was in distress was quite hard to take, especially as the nurse telling me had better eyebrows than me. Basically, I'll be totally honest here, I was hearing what she was saying but I was also wondering when an appropriate time was to ask her how she'd done them. They weren't natural. Those had been enhanced with a god-like cosmetic treatment.

She left us alone for a moment to let it all sink in. Well, I now realize she left because the ward was getting extremely busy but I'd watched too much *Casualty* and so in my head she was leaving us to 'let it all sink in'.

'You look sad,' said Jon. 'What are you thinking?'

'Microblading,' I replied.

'What's that?' he asked, presuming it was some sort of surgical procedure, which it is a bit.

'It's where they tattoo your eyebrows with very fine strokes.'

I decided I was going to try to stay positive. This was my thought process over the next few hours:

'This is a bit rubbish. It's not as relaxing as being at home but at least they can find me a mobile monitor and I can play on the bouncy body ball and don't have to lay back on the bed… What's that? Oh, you've run out of mobile monitors. And I do have to lay back on a bed after months of keeping her in the right position? Well, at least I've got my own room and we can make it as relaxing as possible… What's that? There's a wasp nest in the vent above my bed and they're flying in? Oh well, at least we can move rooms. No? No rooms left. One or two wasps aren't that bad. Ah, shit, a swarm of wasps? Surely they'll move us now… What's that? They've found some hairspray instead and they'll kill the little fuckers with that.'

So I got on my invisible magic carpet (this is the hypno-birthing exercise we learned; I didn't take LSD), put the white bed sheet over my head to keep away the wasps and I stayed calm. I was calm because we could hear her little heartbeat on the monitor and every time Louise the nurse came in to check on me (I later found out they were different nurses and I was calling them all Louise) she commented on how relaxed the baby was and I was, for a first-time proud mother.

She wasn't in distress; I knew she wasn't. I had a little voice in my head, the voice of womanhood, of mother nature, coming from somewhere deep and safe. Or perhaps it was just the voice of the woman in the advert that was a tree (why did she need deodorant?). It said, 'You don't want to be here, you want to be alone, you know what you're doing.' But then you doubt yourself, don't you? Rational thinking kicks in and you remember mothers used to die of this, that they still do.

The voice was still there: 'You can do this on your own.' I shut the mother nature-sounding voice off. I think if I'd had left the voice on we would have had a chat like this:

VOICE:

You should have done this alone in a wood.

ME:

It's just not practical. It's 2016. I saw a YouTube video of a woman doing it in Finland – she had bigger hips than me and I can't squat that long, ask my old PE teacher.

VOICE:

> *Okay hun, just saying, and you've got lovely eyebrows, you don't need to get them tattooed.*

ME:

> *Thanks, I know my eyebrows are fine but hers are better than mine and I think my husband has noticed this on a subconscious level. (The voice didn't really understand this. I think she's from a bygone era.)*

VOICE:

> *Stop calling everyone Louise.*

ME:

> *I'll try.*

VOICE:

> *I know where you can get a good camping stove for that four-man tent he's bought.*

Looking back at the birth is hard. I know Jon was relieved I was at the hospital and I was relieved he was relieved and we didn't know then about the nature of the complications I had so I sucked it up and tried to crack a few jokes to 'Louise'.

It went a bit like this…

After an epidural in my spine (which really *didn't* hurt but I pretended it did as Jon's view of it was a massive needle possibly longer than my leg being pushed into me and I thought, 'I'm going to be able milk this for years') still nothing was happening. And I'm not sure why or when or if people were just confused as to why I was calling them Louise but somewhere in those 26 hours the baby, my baby, went into a posterior position (aka, she was facing backwards) and no one realized and instead I was pumped full of drugs to try to make my cervix dilate and at the last minute someone realized it wasn't going to. Her little head had been hitting my cervix all that time and she was still as cool as a cucumber. I knew she wasn't distressed.

Then something happened quite quickly. The tone in the room between all the Louises changed and we were getting ready for theatre. Jon and I were fading away with tiredness and we couldn't even be bothered to argue. It was clear I had no energy to do any pushing – I don't think I could have even eaten the toast I'd seen them bring out on the TV programme *One Born Every Minute* and I really, really wanted that toast. I'll be honest, I watched a lot of episodes and put up with the screeching Liverpudlian mums and the crying dads in football shirts just to see the toast come out. I pictured myself on a bed with fake tan eating that toast. I pictured it a lot, I could taste it. But while I was thinking about THAT toast, TV toast, Dr Louise said something that made the tiredness end instantly: he said that although my baby was chilling with the good chills, he felt that it could change quickly and we had to get the baby out NOW.

It was an emergency.

I didn't like it, I liked toast.

We haven't wanted to find out in detail what happened next – if they should have checked the position of the baby earlier or if they shouldn't have kept pumping me full of drugs – because they were heroes and when they wheeled us to the theatre the whole team looked exhausted.

Instinct kicked in. I wanted to cheer them up, so I went full 'Bobby Ball'. I was like Mr Blobby or my first night at the London Palladium. My thinking was, 'If I make them laugh they won't let us die,' and it worked. Well, I think it was down to me, I suppose it could have been all their years of medical training.

The other thing I know is soon after that I went a bit Pete Tong. My rational thinking went – which I know it's meant to at some point, as it's why you buy 'mum jeans' and suddenly really like Elton John and you cry at yogurt adverts. As they injected me with a massive hit of drugs to numb me from neck to toes before I went into theatre, I really felt I wouldn't be able to take another big hit of it and I was right.

I caused a right scene. Imagine – it was like walking off that Palladium stage to a standing ovation and then coming back on and telling them they're all a bunch of twats. I completely lost it. I couldn't swallow, which really freaked me out, but in retrospect perhaps that was because they'd numbed my tongue. I couldn't move any of my body and I was sure they'd given me too much and then I started to feel like I was going to go unconscious, which must have been when I was losing a lot of blood.

I thought I was going to die! I mean, in truth, I wasn't because they had me hooked up to equipment that told them I was okay but I *thought* I was going to die and what was worse was that I convinced Jon I was going to die. At that moment he turned a greyer shade of grey and he's still that colour now if I'm honest.

Then my eyesight clouded over. I had double vision and as they pulled my baby out, I told Jon I couldn't hold on and I wanted to see her. I burst out crying because I couldn't make her out properly and nurse Louise wasn't really doing enough to console us. I think she was busy doing something more important.

Jon did not know what was going on. The job now was to stitch me up quickly, so no one explained to him that I would be okay and I *was* okay, I was more than okay.

Whatever we feel about how that had gone, all the Louises did their jobs amazingly. Tired and overworked, and seriously under-staffed and under-paid, in a busy hospital building with state-of-the-art equipment, on a warm summer's night, they made sure we were both fine and I got to take home something that suddenly made life seem worthwhile and is currently making me feel love and tiredness in ways I never thought possible. Who knew love and needing to sleep were so closely connected?

That nurse deserved to have perfect eyebrows.

This next bit is really weird.

They wheeled me out of the theatre and took me to like a holding bay. I could only see out of a tiny bit of my left eye but –

and there's no other way to say this, really – I could make out this *really*, *really* young, sexy Italian male nurse as he took hold of one of my breasts (finally someone touched them!) and stuck my baby on the end of it.* At last I could stroke my baby. She looked angry and red and was very hungry. Her face was all screwed up but she was sucking away like mad.

There she was. It was like waiting nine months outside of a rock god's house hoping to catch a glimpse, knowing you're their biggest fan, and when you do it's like slow motion, it's not real, time stands still and it's familiar and alien and confusing and you don't know if you're feeling everything or nothing at all.

I thought about Jon. Poor Jon – can you imagine? He started out a day ago buying a four-man tent, went through hours of confusion, thought he'd lost his wife, was handed a baby – who I might add looked him straight in the eye as if to say, 'Where the F is that magic carpet you've been banging on about, mate?' – and was now being instructed to go home straight away 'to get some rest' and leave me with this Adonis who had my left tit in his hand. If that's not going to make you stop at a petrol station and buy a bottle of cheap whisky, I don't know what is.

I was so upset. I couldn't see my baby clearly, I couldn't take her in. I couldn't lift her to me, I couldn't drown out the noise and lay skin to skin but what I could do was let the little tinker breastfeed and oh boy, did we breastfeed. She didn't come off it. She was like a racehorse, on your marks go, her little mouth

---

* Jon – He was not called Louise!

doing a crazy sucking motion. I was amazed she knew what to do, like she'd been practising in there. I was so glad I'd gone to the classes, knowing how to stuff it in her mouth the correct way was a load off – nipple to nose, wait for her mouth to open and then shove it in and off she goes! The only trouble was when I went to take the tit away again she'd cry and I decided that crying was bad and I think that is why, a week later, she won't let me put her down and wants to feed all the time and sleep on my shoulder like a chihuahua.

Basically, that night I just let her feed and feed and feed and I got no sleep and a very matronly dinner-lady-type nurse – not really a Louise, more a Pat or Sandra – came in and told me off and said I needed to get some sleep. She took my bundle of shrivelled joy away with her down the corridor. She looked so tiny on her shoulder and when they left it really felt she'd taken a part of me away. I suppose she had. I tried to sleep but I heard a baby crying down the corridor and I was sure it was mine and that she was frightened and needed me.

I don't know how I managed it but I got out of bed and walked out of the door, which is forbidden after a C-section until the next day. I walked down the corridor, not able to stand up straight, as it feels like they've tried to sew your top and bottom half together like a sandwich, which is a very weird feeling. (I think I thought they stitched the surface area for some reason, like if you cut your head open. I didn't realize you have other layers of stitches inside too.) Everyone heals differently and can walk at different times. The nurse's eyes popped out of her head when she saw me and, while I was expecting some sort of Mum of the Year sticker, she was horrified that I'd come to reclaim my flesh and bones.

Anyway, I got my baby back and we carried on feeding away and I didn't get any sleep and that's why I kept seeing things move out of the corner of my eye. (My eyesight came back the next day, by the way.)

Now I know that of course I should have slept and if someone who you trust is willing to hold your baby while you sleep, you just let them, okay? YOU LET THEM. Last night I was particularly tired and it did cross my mind to go back to the hospital ward and ask the nurse if she would like to hold her again and I could just sleep behind her desk by her feet or something. Or maybe I could sleep on her other shoulder and she could rock us both?

I didn't get any toast, though.

HOME

When we got home from the hospital I had to hobble into the house via the side door as the front door had steps. I felt like a collapsed deckchair that had been hit by a bus. I hadn't seen anyone look as bad as me in their first pictures of mum and baby – no one.

My mum was there, as Jon had given her our house key so she could let herself in and she'd spent two days making food for us, stuff we could reheat. She really went to town; there was no way we could eat, reheat or freeze the volume of food she'd made. I think she'd panicked because she was worrying about me. We knew my mum is best in these sorts of emotionally charged situations if she's given a task to do. She is an amazing cook but something bizarre happened and possibly all her emotions came out in the cooking. There were some odd assortments.

I think I threw her a curveball when she said, 'What do you want?' and I said, 'I'm not sure, I've been drinking a lot of custard.'

I don't think I should have told her I was drinking custard; it was a red rag to a bull as my mother is a feeder. We come from a long line of feeders but I get it now, there is nothing that gives you more satisfaction than watching your child eat. She found it very hard to see me in a mess and it was difficult for her at first to focus on my baby when *her* baby looked so rough.

My mum gave me the biggest hug and I mentioned to her softly that she needed to put a bra on if she was wearing a vest in our house. My mother left after that and visited five churches in the local area.

I was so ecstatic that I had this healthy baby at home with us. So why did I feel so sad?

I didn't feel very feminine, very womanly. I should have been able to cope better and bounce out of there; my husband shouldn't be looking ashen-faced with a new grey tinge and worried eyes – I felt like he was worried because I didn't know what I was doing. Probably none of these things were true but that's how I felt. I thought that when my little baby wasn't breastfeeding she looked at me like she was angry and tense. Jon said baby Elsie looked like the Psammead from that weird film that no one has watched all the way through. I think it's called *Five Children and It*.

The truth was, it felt like something was missing, or not quite whole, like being unsatisfied after a meal you'd waited all day for. I had a feeling deep in my tummy, a sadness that I couldn't express but everyone could see. None of us could relax because of it – my mum and Jon could see I was distant, I think. Jon stepped in, he took control, he did everything. He was panicked but his maternal side sort of kicked in.

I took a shower and it felt like when they have showers in movies – obviously not in any way sexual, not even to those weirdos who like pregnant women, more like the showers they take after they've come back from battle. The warm water touching my skin and washing away everything that felt surgical and monitored was such a welcome relief. I was trying to transform into a mum I'd seen on the nappy adverts, the mums I'd seen in those wonderful photos of mum and baby on Facebook – tired eyes but glowing skin, shiny hair that they'd manage to put a brush through. How I'd pictured it all. The Fairy liquid advert with the soft hands.

The shower wasn't long enough. Our baby girl was crying and I needed to get to her.

THE NIGHT FEED

I'm finding the night feeds hard. I feel lonely in the middle of the night. I get a sinking feeling when it gets to the evening. And that's not to say I don't love, adore and cherish my baby. In a way, I think I still can't believe my luck. I just can't quite take her in and I want to hide away for a bit. Is that okay, to feel like that?

I think my body is still in complete shock from the emergency C-section, if I'm honest. There just wasn't the after-care. I was fast-tracked out of hospital and I'm sure that's a) because they felt I could manage and b) because I wasn't poorly enough to stay in. But I didn't feel ready. Someone told me that years ago, if you had a C-section they'd keep you in hospital for up to two weeks.

A nurse came over to our house and she asked me to fill in a questionnaire to see if I was depressed. I lied to make me sound happier. I knew I should be honest but I also didn't see what they could offer me. What I really wanted was the body of a 21-year-old and to be on a beach in Ibiza, in the 'quiet' part of the island on some sort of sexy retreat. I've never been abroad and come back in a god-like state. I've come back needing a holiday. But they tell me that young people go away now and drink juice and do yoga.

You see, even though I'd never now want to be without this little bundle of joy and nothing could take me away from her, I guess I do need a bit of time away just to heal and sleep and that's not going to happen. I wonder when I can realistically go away by myself? Jon looks like he's just got back from war, he's definitely still in shock. He sometimes makes us both a burger with real cow in it and passes it off as just being tired.

I feel like I've sort of gone somewhere else mentally and my body is in charge now. My milk leaks when my baby cries and my boobs fill up again while she sleeps. My body tells me what to eat and drink and if I don't listen I dehydrate. I need so much water and fat to make milk. It's so weird. I do feel sad and low but I also feel so needed – someone totally depends on me and that feels great. I'm looking forward to just feeling happy and grateful – these mixed emotions are weird, man!

I tell you what, though, I'm proud I'm still breastfeeding. My mum and my granny were not able to do this. I'd set myself a goal that if I could breastfeed for two weeks I could do it until she was 23.

THE BREAST PUMP

Now, let me tell you something: the thing that has most annoyed me about the birth/hospital not going my way thing isn't the wasp nest or the double vision or the unplanned C-section, it is what happened yesterday.

Yesterday marks two and half weeks since the birth and I needed a breast pump. I'm going to attempt to siphon off enough breast milk so that it can go into a bottle and Jon can do a night feed because quite simply when it gets to about 6pm a wave of bitter depression and dread that I'm going to have to 'do the night' comes over me. Luckily there's Facebook and all the natural mother websites to go to for advice. One website in particular has a helpline for new mums that are breastfeeding. I rang it yesterday crying, saying I can't sleep because she won't let me put her down, and the woman – she sounded like she was probably called Camilla or something and once lived in Richmond, the super-posh area just down the road from us – said that my baby thinks a sabre-toothed tiger is going to get her. I explained we lived in Surbiton and she said that she's programmed to the Ice Age. I put the phone down and cursed the middle classes.

This same website that also has the emergency phone line told me not to introduce a bottle straight away as the baby will have nipple confusion. The baby has not got nipple confusion, she knows the bottle is a plastic tit and plastic tits are rubbish but anyway, I want to try again and I want to get the milk out, so we went back to the hospital to get an industrial-sized breast pump.

While we waited at reception and had a little argument (Jon keeps telling me my breastfeeding position isn't right), a young woman floated out of the maternity ward, thanked the reception desk and left with the most perfectly formed baby in a basket.

The lady, I would argue, in any social setting around the world, would make you look at yourself self-consciously: long tanned legs, an expensive summer dress at a modest length, silken hair brushing her shoulders. I had the rage, and I needed to know.

I marched/hobbled up to the reception in my Polish daywear, which I think we established was intended *not* to be in any way modest or demure and I asked, 'Was that lady a sister or a relative of a mother on the ward?'

'No, she's just had her baby, she was so lovely,' the nurse on reception replied.

'Where did she get her blow-dry from?' I asked jokingly, but not jokingly.

'She's young!' the nurse said.

Bitch. I'm young.

I felt cheated. I am dehydrated. My skin looks like a dinosaur's. I keep asking people, 'Do I look like a dinosaur?'

What hurt me the most was they obviously have two exits: she'd gone out of the public door, the one they wanted you to see, and I was basically let out the back door into a loading bay and Jon had to pull the car up as close as he could. I had struggled to put one foot in front of the other.

And then there was something else I was even more miffed about, seriously miffed about. My hypno-birthing teacher. I obviously do not in any way advocate violence, I live for peace and all that, but sometimes, in the darkest hours of the night, given what I now know, I picture being driven up to her house, ringing her bell and slapping her around the face. She had four kids and took money off me – she knew full well you can't 'breathe' a baby out.

But then it struck me like a lightning bolt – was that the reason my baby had kept so calm through it all? Because I was calm on my magic carpet? Maybe I didn't do so badly after all.

I sent my hypno-birthing teacher a thank you note:

> *Dear Louise,*
> *All went well but not as expected: the magic carpet was delayed slightly and although it wasn't a smooth journey the destination was well worth the wait. Thank you. I think the passenger was very grateful for the calmness.*
>
> *You didn't breathe four kids out, did you? I want my money back, you lying cow.*

I haven't sent it yet.

MOTHER AND BABY MASSAGE

It's been two months now since Elsie was born and I still can't walk very well or pick things up and my complexion still looks grey. I'm weepy of an evening just before I have to start the night feeds and I feel very unattractive and, well, 'floopy'. I'm having to wear shoes that I've only ever seen old people wear when they dance on cruise ships: they've got a bit of sparkle but they are designed for support. But my baby is putting on weight and the midwife says she's doing well so none of this actually matters. BUT I am knackered because she's not a sleeper (the baby, not the midwife).

So imagine my joy when I see an advert for a mother and baby massage. I was delighted. I dusted myself off, and baby and I waddled there. My hips and shoulders were killing me and my arms still hadn't strengthened enough for the long breastfeeds (they keep saying to use a pillow but I can never get the latch in the right position...) but what happiness to know I now had a weekly massage session! I imagined on my walk there that someone must watch your baby or you have your baby next to you while you had a massage. I wondered if you then went to lie down with a blanket over you like those weird yoga sessions where you come out more tired than when you went in.

I arrived at the session a bit late but I joined the group. I then noticed three things:

 All the mothers were taller than me.

They all had Bugaboo prams.

Oh, and YOU massage the FUCKING BABIES!

Excuse my French. I adore and love and cherish and have soothed and delicately handled my baby, of course I have. I would rather go through any amount of pain to make sure this little angel who relies on me completely is not in discomfort – please don't get me wrong – but she doesn't do anything, she literally hasn't done *anything*, she is held most of the day as she doesn't like being put down. I NEED THE MASSAGE!

I wedged myself next to the bolshiest woman I could find. I was pissed off and didn't want to be next to someone who makes her own bath bombs. We were being shown how to massage their feet. I laid baby Elsie down on the mat and she looked up at me as if to say, 'Where on earth are we and why are you touching my feet with a weird look on your face?' She then cried and everyone looked at me like I was a witch. Eventually, she settled and I got the attention of the moody mum next to me.

'They should be massaging us, not the babies!' I said.

'Excuse me?'

'Mother and baby massaging, y'know, I thought *I'd* be getting the massage,' I explained.

'I don't follow. Are you Dutch?' she said.

I reminded myself I was in Surbiton in Surrey. To be successfully humorous in a Hull accent here requires finding a specific kind of person, usually someone who has gone to university in Leeds.

I did the massage class in stages in between the crying and needing to change nappies. I got a room full of sympathetic looks. For some reason, my baby was the only one actually doing baby things. 'They've all bored theirs,' I imagined. We left early and I got a bag of chips on the way home. How many days have been saved by a bag of chips? Too many to count.

MY MOTHER RETURNS

My mother is back visiting, she's cooking some meals for us and pretending we might have once said we eat meat, which we don't. Well, Jon doesn't. I was allowed to but now I'm not pregnant I feel bad about it.

Today Jon was too tired to battle with my mother, who is completely manipulating the situation in order to feed us dead animals. She has a spring in her step that Jon has agreed to eat a dead cow. I gave her 'a look', which she clocked and said, 'Lucy, it's not a full dead cow, it's just the mince part of the cow. It's good because nothing is wasted.'

Jon is still trying to show me how to breastfeed. He keeps telling me I've not got the angle right – he's had one plastic doll on his imaginary tit for 20 seconds and he thinks he's bloody Old Mother Hubbard. (I'm not recommending having 20 kids and living in a shoe.)

We all settled down to watch TV.

Jon said he didn't want our baby to watch TV.

I said, 'What do you mean? She's a newborn, she won't watch TV!' I looked down at her in my arms and lo and behold she was cranking her neck in an uncomfortable position so she could watch TV. Every time I faced her towards me she kept doing it again.

'It's the bright light she likes, it won't do her any harm,' my mum said.

Jon was worried about her looking at the bright lights so he angled her away so she couldn't see it at all.

'I don't think they're meant to want to watch TV at this age; she's only two months old!' I said.

Little Elsie started to cry. Jon and I both tried to soothe her: nothing, it didn't work.

My mum picked her up and put her on her lap and she stopped instantly. Elsie stared into her eyes, into her glasses, and smiled at her, mesmerized by Mum. Mum wept with joy, overwhelmed by the wonderful connection she had with her granddaughter. It was incredible, we'd never seen Elsie so focused before – it was truly something to behold... Then we realized all at the same time: SHE WAS WATCHING THE TV IN THE REFLECTION ON MY MUM'S GLASSES.

DRINKING CUSTARD

I'm still breastfeeding. Elsie is three months old now and still putting on weight. I'm eating lots of flapjacks and I'm not sorry to say that still nothing quenches my thirst like custard from a tetra pack; it's making such lovely healthy breast milk.

I feel like an athlete, I do. Breastfeeding is an extreme sport. In the morning when I've done a full day and a night of breastfeeding and I'm ready to face another day, I feel like someone who's climbed Kilimanjaro or successfully returned to Everest base camp. To think that there are some women in the world who have breastfed *and* have climbed mountains…my word, and we think men are the tough ones! I have a new-found power, a super strength, I'm kick ass.

The other night, when Elsie wouldn't settle ALL night, we drove her around and around in the car while I sat next to her car seat and pulled my breast over to her mouth, like a stretchy version of the bionic woman. (Is there such a thing? I'm not into sci-fi.) And would you believe it? The kid didn't want the one nearest to her, oh no, she wanted my right breast. I let her suckle and eventually she fell asleep. She was exhausted and I needed custard.

I made Jon stop at an Esso garage and just as I got out, he said the worst thing any man could ever say to a woman who has just climbed a mountain. He said, 'Your right tit is hanging out.'

I swivelled my head towards him, like a dinosaur, and said, 'Fuck you.'

I marched across that forecourt like a woman scorned. The men standing around and coming out of the shop stopped what they were doing one by one to look at me.

'Yes,' I said, 'this is a breastfeeding tit. I have been awake all night stretching it over a car seat into the mouth of a baby that has not slept for more than three hours in a row since it came into the world. It is not an attractive sight, it's like a working seaside donkey and it's empty. It is sagging like the last-ever Roman centurion – it was once in action and now it's just limp. Take a good look. This is what breast meat really looks like, this is real.'

I mean, that's what I wanted to say. What I actually said was: 'What are you looking at? Buy some socks.' Then I folded my breast back in my bra, like a tablecloth. Yes, just like that.

A man in front of me in the queue asked if I wanted a Creme Egg. I said no, I'm okay with my tin of custard. He gave me a sympathetic look. I know that face by now. We got back in the car and all the way home I wished I'd said yes to that Creme Egg.

The next evening, both still shattered from 'tit gate', we had a Chinese takeaway for our tea. I thought to myself how clever I was for managing to eat it with my fork in one hand while I held my baby with the other arm so she could breastfeed. Then I looked down and saw half my noodles were on my daughter's little baby head. I took this as a good omen. My body looks different and I haven't been able to wear any of my normal clothes, my social life is non-existent and the house looks like they're having a refit at Mothercare, but at least I know that I'm still the same person. The old Lucy would drop noodles on her baby's head and it was good to know the type of mother I was going to be – angry and impulsive, messy but loving.

Today was the day I started her on solids. I was so nervous. It felt like when you give a horse a Polo and the moment before its big teeth and tongue tickle your hand you think, 'Oh, shit is it a Polo I'm meant to give them? Is it hay, or a carrot?'

I tried her on baby porridge first but it was too hot so I let it cool down. Then I tried her on a second bowl of porridge… I'm only joking. She spat the porridge out. Not wanting to be deterred, I tried her on blitzed kale – a mental thing to do but I had read that some babies love it and it sort of gets their taste buds ready for, well, living with Gwyneth Paltrow, I suppose.

She was disgusted by the kale, disgusted with me, disgusted with life. In fact, a small amount of trust had been tainted. I'd been giving her the sweet milky nectar of the gods on tap for a full four-and-a-half months and then I make a big song and dance of bowls and spoons and whip out KALE! I mean, adults only started eating kale a few years ago, it was practically a weed before then. Next was carrots. Yes, she liked that – 'That'll do, if you must,' her face sort of said. This course was then followed by peas, which again were satisfactory for her.

Then I gave her a little bit of my mash. BLOODY RESULT. Her face said it all – 'Why have you been keeping this from me, woman?'

I like people that like mash.

We're going to get on well, me and this kid.

EVEN MORE ABOUT TITS

We're both loving the solids but the breastfeeding is still in first place. Due to how well I'm doing with a little help from the best sucker in town (my baby, not my husband) I am thinking of writing a book about BREASTFEEDING. I've put breastfeeding in capital letters as I think it should always be in capitals because it a very epic thing to do; it is hardcore. The book is going to be called *BREASTFEEDING*.

This will be my intro:

> *Dear reader,*
>
> *I have collated here the highs and lows of BREASTFEEDING.*
>
> *BREASTFEEDING, quite frankly, second after childbirth and putting together a French dresser from Ikea, is the hardest and most wonderful thing I've ever had to do.*
>
> *It represents life itself: joy and pain. Though there shouldn't be any pain if you're BREASTFEEDING, it means they haven't latched on right. You need some guidance with it but don't give up for that reason. There are lots of other reasons why you might need/want to stop but don't let this be the one. I actually found YouTube*

> *videos about latching on very useful. There are some*
> *French ones that made me feel rather cosmopolitan*
> *(while I wept in the middle of the night with one breast*
> *hanging out).*

I think I'll have to put a note in the book to say that the main reason for writing it, if I do manage to write it, is my frustration that scientists (I bet they're male scientists) are spending lots and lots of money and resources to investigate if breast milk is better than formula and lo and behold they have found that it is. Some of them were surprised by just how many benefits breast milk has and in fact breast milk is so complex that they're only really beginning to understand its properties. Well, no shit, Sherlock.

> *This is why the Native Americans worshipped women,*
> *why in some cultures women were seen as godlike,*
> *why birth and lactating were something everyone was*
> *involved in and mothers were pampered and cherished*
> *and brought gifts and cooked for. Of course breast milk*
> *is special. It's made in a place close to the heart and it*
> *changes to meet the needs of the child – if a child is sick it*
> *knows, or if a child is just using it for comfort it won't be*
> *as fatty, or if they're having a growth spurt it'll be thicker.*

I hate to say it but it's a bit like custard. You know you get the white, thick posh custard and the thin one out of the packet? It's the same, it's made from the heart. Custard is love, just like breast milk.

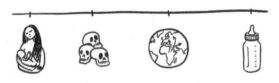

100BC or whatever: woman breastfeeds and keeps babies alive. Then, along the line, all the different huge events: plagues and stuff, mass migration. 'Still they've kept babies alive'. Then in 1973 or something a group of scientists think there might actually be something going on with breast milk; it's as if it's keeping babies alive. From this time after, men think 'hmm, we need to invent our own form of breast milk, let's put it in a bottle.'

My granny couldn't breastfeed, my mum said, so she had a wet nurse. No bottle or plastic. I think a lot of women wouldn't like the idea of another woman breastfeeding their baby. I'm not one of those but isn't it sad? We all know we've lost touch with nature, we've seen the memes on social media about it – this is a glowing example for me.

I stopped writing at this point as the worthiness was clouding my eyes. And I got a call from a friend of mine. She has FOUR kids and she told me very breezily on the phone that she breastfed two of them till they were three (THREE?!) and the second two she gave a bottle to. Guess what, the bloody bottle-fed ones never get ill and they slept better and she could drink throughout. So FUCK YOU nature and fuck you breastfeeding book.

I'm going to watch *Location, Location, Location* and buy stuff I don't need off Amazon.

MY MOTHER RETURNS...AGAIN

I am so tired. If I put the baby down she just cries so we now take it in turns to hold the baby. Really the baby only sleeps after a huge feed at about 10pm and I have to wrap her in swaddling so she thinks she's being held and slowly move my hands away. It sometimes takes a few attempts. So we asked my mother if she wanted to stay. She did and was concerned about how tired we were. She told me to put brandy on a dummy and give it to baby Elsie – 'That's what granny gave you, Lucy.' This explains why

I'm five-foot-one and all the other women in the family are five-foot-five. That, and the fact we lived above a dry cleaners.

Mum also took the opportunity to not wear a bra again. I said she was taking liberties as we were both too tired and too fragile to argue with her. I must explain, it's not just about the bra, it's that usually there will be more inappropriate behaviour to follow. She also asked Jon if he knew if I had any Vagisil wash she could use. I wouldn't mind but I was sitting right next to him. Vagisil is an intimate wash primarily for women over 55 but it doesn't want to be seen like that. I think it would prefer younger women to use it too. Honestly, she's getting worse every time we see her.

We then had a takeaway on our laps while we watched TV, Jon and I a bit dazed and spaced out. Halfway through eating, my mum took off her bra and put it on the coffee table next to my husband. (When you're older if you get a bit full and you take your bra off, you can eat more. That's something to look forward to, isn't it?) Well, Jon went white as a sheet. It was a bloody big bra too. My mother saw his face and she slapped him around the chops with it, saying, 'Ooh gerr over yourself, it's from Marks & Spencer!'

I can tell that Mum thinks we are being ridiculous with the baby and tiring ourselves out unnecessarily. Jon still looks grey. But then she rested tiny baby Elsie against her neck and that was it! She offered to do the mornings for us which basically means taking the baby at about 6am so I can sleep.

My mum has never felt so relaxed. When she brings baby Elsie downstairs and rests her little sleeping body on her chest she enters a meditative state. There is nothing more relaxing than a sleeping baby.

I think a lot of things when my baby is asleep. I think how hard it must be to be a new single mum and how little support some mums get and how lucky I am. Jackie, my dear friend, is a single mum. She's a warrior really, all single parents are. Maybe you have to be a child of one to fully understand this or maybe you just being left with a baby might do the trick.

I've got one more week before Jon starts warming up for his comedy show. He's not going to be away a lot – just a few nights a week and they're close by too – but I'm literally petrified. I can't imagine being left alone with my baby and it's saddening to me that I feel like this. This nest needs to open its doors; Jon has to go and pick up twigs from the outside world and I need to learn how to survive.

TONGUE TIE

Something hasn't felt right for a while. It felt like the baby wasn't ever relaxing, like she was in pain – nothing extreme but sort of uncomfortable.

To cut a long story short, she has tongue tie. It's posterior tongue tie and basically it stops the tongue sticking out. We all have a little bit of skin that attaches our tongue to the base of our mouth, it's just that Elsie's is quite thick and she can't really reach her teeth. She certainly can't stick her tongue out, bless her. Although she's feeding well and putting on the right amount of weight for a five-month-old she might be working a lot harder to get milk and latch on and this could be why she's very, very grumpy. As I understand it, the tongue has to sort of gently lap the nipple when breastfeeding, like a woodland creature, but the tongue tie could be giving her trapped wind and, as we all know, sometimes when you have trapped wind you can think you've punctured an internal organ.

In the old days, a midwife would keep one nail long (and clean, you'd hope) and cut the tongue tie at birth. I don't know if this is true but the more I tell people the more I think it's not true, like my interesting fact about ancient Egyptians: when their cats died they shaved off their eyebrows the next morning. I suppose that shows how conspiracy theories work – someone has a mental idea, like 'Bill Gates infected the world with Covid-19', and the first few people you tell, you REALLY, really mean it, and so they go off and tell people and then you tell a couple more people but now you're not so sure anymore. By that time, though, there are loads of really mental people with a mental idea and it spreads just like a virus – the virus of human gullibility. (Just to be clear, BILL GATES DID NOTHING OF THE SORT.)

We took Elsie to a private clinic as the NHS doesn't seem so bothered about tongue tie. I did wonder if we should be but the doctor thought it might help. When I say private, it is accredited by the NHS. It was in quite a random place, though, somewhere we'd never heard of before but still only a few miles from where we live. It was one of those market towns that looks like it should be by the sea but isn't. It had a Bonmarché and Greggs in the centre and lots of people on electric wheelchairs with dogs on their lap.

The women conducting the snipping of the tongue tie were all lovely – ex-midwives with lovely blow-dried hair and they still smelled of the air freshener they have at home. Feeders too, I bet. They told me it won't hurt as there are no nerve endings in the tongue tie and the cry will just be the shock of it. I couldn't handle it so I let Jon hold her while they did it. Poor Jon, he was white when he brought her back around the corner. Elsie's cry was piercing and I really wondered if we'd made the right choice – perhaps we should have left it?

The next few hours were some of the worst. It took Elsie such a long time to be able to control her tongue as it was now sort of loose in her mouth and she was frustrated, she had to learn how to feed all over again. It got to the evening and Jon said he had to leave for his gig. I was in bits but he couldn't cancel, he was performing to a full house of people. I felt so vulnerable and useless but I pulled it together and gave myself a good talking to.

Eventually, Elsie started to feed okay again. Gosh, I hope we did the right thing. Parenting is hard, man!

I looked it up again on the internet, which was almost like torturing myself as there seemed to be two camps about how effective it is. Oh gosh, and we put her through the shock if it. What if she remembers? What if it is stored in her body somewhere; what if it all comes out when she's a teenager and she turns into a goth? What if she gets really into archaeology? Or maybe she'll learn to play flute and keep growing her hair until it trails on the floor? Maybe she'll collect miniature models of snails? You just don't know how things will affect young people.

I suppose the next few days will tell us if it was the right thing to do. Hopefully she might seem more comfortable. Gosh, what a new feeling this is – guilt, angst, nervousness. I was told about this by the elders in my village called Hull. They said that you NEVER, never stop worrying. Ahh, I get why people with kids look so old and haggard now!

These first six months have been such a mix of emotions. We have the smiliest baby I've ever seen, and cheeky too, and although the breastfeeding is hard I have loved those snuggly moments. But she still just will not sleep for more than three hours in a row. I've done loads of all-nighters in the past so I thought not sleeping would be easier than this. But it's just not quite the same as Leeds Festival, is it?

I love this cheeky, chubby, bubbly pudding of joy very, very, very much. It really is unconditional and all that – but she will not nap either. I mean, she *will* nap but I have to be holding her in a rocking motion. And she needs naps – whoah! Does she need naps! The only way she'll sleep not in my arms is if she's being pushed in the pram. I do this twice a day. The other problem is she'll wake up and go batshit if I stop the pram, so I'm currently walking for two hours a day after having interrupted sleep.

It makes sense – this is why I was drinking custard, to stock up on calories for sleep-deprived walking. I really wish I had a designer pram for this walking. Also, everything I've ever thought about child rearing is coming undone. All these mums and dads that I've seen throughout my life on a nice jolly walk pushing a pram on the way to pick up fresh bread or visit Auntie Jean, well, they're not, are they? They're not doing it for themselves, they're just pushing a pram around aimlessly so their baby doesn't turn into the devil.

Also, you know that lovely image we've all seen of the kid snuggled on his fit dad's shoulder, still holding his balloon, as if they've had this amazing day out at Disney World or somewhere and the kid has fallen asleep in a bubble of sleepy joy? I've just realized that's a fiction too. In reality, that kid has had a massive fucking meltdown, had to be taken away from the e-numbers and flashing lights and has crashed out in utter exhaustion.

And Fairy liquid has never made your hands soft, has it?

This is so hard. Especially knowing that I've been lied to all these years.

SIX MONTHS OLD (HALF A YEAR! WE MADE IT TO HALF A YEAR!!)

I had one of those moments tonight when I sort of looked down on myself and thought, 'OH GOD, WHAT ARE YOU DOING?'

I've been fortunate enough to have a lot of these moments. I say fortunate because I think it's great I'm able to see them for what they are. I can reflect on them and they also must be very character-building. In fact, Jon said the other day that I was intimidating! Well, what actually happened was that I said that one of the mums at playgroup acts like I'm intimidating and Jon replied, 'You are intimidating.' Of all the things he's ever said to me this one has definitely pleased me the most.

So. This 'moment' I had. Elsie had napped late in the morning so her afternoon nap was late and fell over tea-time. I was on my own with her and started pushing the pram around the streets aimlessly, nodding to a couple of 20-something girls who probably thought I was having a little jolly walk to somewhere. They looked into the pram and my daughter, with her eyes half closed, gave them a very gummy smile and they sort of screamed in delight. Part of me wanted to stop them and show them the state of my body underneath my lovely polyester and elastic Polish clothes and tell them I hadn't had more than three hours of sleep in a row for six months.

Just after this, the breastfeeding hunger hit me and I realized that I hadn't eaten all day. In fact, I hadn't even washed or brushed my teeth (but I had managed to put on blusher and concealer, I'm not an animal). You have to eat and drink a lot when you're breastfeeding – your body is a factory and cannot be left unattended. However, once my daughter is in the pram you cannot stop the pram, you cannot pause the pram and you cannot even go back on yourself. And once she's awoken angry and disappointed with your efforts, she won't go back to sleep again. She'll ruin you.

But I had a cunning plan.

While still pushing the crap red pram, I managed to order a Deliveroo. I timed my route perfectly to coincide with the delivery driver arriving; it was sheer precision, like a military operation.

I approached the house as the driver got off his bike. I saw him pick up my chicken with mash, gravy, a side of peas and a chocolate pudding, and, just as he turned to walk up to my front door, I politely snatched it from his hand. I walked off at the same consistent pace, without breaking stride, and I mouthed back to him: 'I'm pushing the child of Satan, do not approach me.'

Mission accomplished.

RASPBERRIES

My mother has come to visit again to help me while Jon is away. Elsie has started to want to reach out and grab things so we've put a little play gym bar above her with dangly things on. It's wonderful to watch. My mum was changing Elsie's nappy and she could see she was so close to touching a little lion… Mum waited but Elsie didn't manage to grab it so she picked her up and took her through to the living room. Well, the noises that came out of Elsie! I rushed downstairs. Elsie's little baby face was all screwed up in my mum's arms, her fists clenched, and my mum was somewhat in shock.

'I think I know what she wants,' my mum said. She put her back on the changing table and Elsie reached out and grabbed the little dangly lion. She pulled it in close to her and didn't let it go. She smiled and cooed; we cried and clapped. Then me and Mum looked at each other.

'By heck, she's got a temper on her this one,' said Mum.

I nodded. 'Yep, but she's not going to get messed around.'

'You know who she's like, don't you?' my mum said.

'Granny,' we both said at the same time.

My granny died when I was 11 but we keep the memory of her alive. It was a passing that shook and uprooted our family as it does in many families when you lose the head of the family, your matriarch. I felt it intensely because she took such an active role in my life. I lived at my grandparents' until I started school and then spent nearly every weekend and holiday there. Granny was a wonderful, strong, formidable, loving woman who had fun and loved a party. She came from the fishing community of Hull and grew up with three big protective brothers. She was a home maker and loved textiles and art. She was beautiful but you could get on the wrong side of her. She adored me and I think and talk about her lot. I can't believe she didn't get to see this part of my life but I feel blessed that my grandad has, as he's a special one too. They don't make men like my grandad any more; no one will ever hold a candle to him. I am so lucky to have had such special grandparents.

I saw Nana, my dad's mum, very rarely as she lived in north London, but when I did she'd be so excited to see me and show me off to all her friends. Oh boy, was I loved and spoilt by her! Though it was just so far away from where we lived and I missed my mum when I was down there and had to go back early. I think you can learn too late how precious grandparents are. I love to see grandparents drink up their grandchildren, like time has stopped. They know the clock is ticking and childhood is a gift, they know the little things are important – the smelling flowers together, feeding the ducks, painting a picture. It's precious because none of it lasts as long as it should do.

Every day it feels like Elsie is making huge strides; we're just blown away by how determined and clever she is. I know you shouldn't ever judge your child by their milestones, or where they are or aren't compared to other babies. It's so sad when parents feel they have to do that. But I can't help but love how our little angel is so aware of everything and everyone – the rolling, the reaching, the holding, the pure joy she seems to have every day.

I don't know if fixing the tongue tie worked or it's just her personality coming out more but what a happy baby she is now! She has really mellowed I think and what a clever, cheeky baby we have. And those eyes! Those piercing blue eyes. She will forever more have us wrapped around her finger and we just mostly spend every day tired and happy.

I do have one question though…Elsie is blowing raspberries. IS THIS NORMAL? No, you don't understand, not in that cute baby way – she's telling me off using raspberries. She's itching to communicate. I think she knows we can talk and she can't and I really get the impression it's driving her nuts. The raspberries are so loud, so sort of…guttural. Yesterday I didn't feel I could take her into Waitrose, I just didn't know what people would think. The issue is also that she's doing it *all day*. She's sort of, well, I know this sounds weird but I think she's bullying me a bit. I feel a little controlled. Her biggest raspberries are when I tidy away her toys or don't let her face the TV, so I've given up. We sat and watched *Homes Under the Hammer* together and she didn't blow one raspberry until I got up to get a drink and stood in front of the TV.

It's like living with a grumpy old man.

TEETHING

Last Christmas I was early in my pregnancy and this Christmas we visited Jon's mum with a drooling, red-cheeked seven-month-old monster who looked really cute in her little red dress and headband and booties. However, our baby is teething like a Trojan. I have never seen a baby teething this much, it feels more as if a shark is teething. She's in so much pain with it, she's biting on anything and everything.

Christmas was actually a bit of a nightmare. Elsie was so fed up. Everyone tried to have a go at comforting her only to pass her back to me like a hot potato. I breastfed around the clock and managed to eat my Christmas dinner one-handed in the 20 minutes or so that she napped. Luckily I had put her in an elf onesie so at least she still looked cute.

At one point, I sat her on Jon's knee and went to take a picture of the cuteness overload. She grabbed his hand to her mouth, picked out his index finger and shoved it in her gob, running her sore gums up and down it like it was a mouth organ. It was one of those moments you'll always remember. I understand why people have a second baby. I can totally see how, in a year's time, I'll forget all the emotional stuff and just remember her playing Jon's finger like it was a mouth organ, dressed as an elf and I'll want another child.

Luckily I've got documented evidence that this is a trap. I will never have another baby.

THE PATRIARCHY

Elsie has just said 'da-da'. I looked it up and it's easier to say than 'ma-ma'. Phew, for a minute I thought the breastfeeding around the clock, the C-section and carrying her for nine months had gone unappreciated!

It's fine to say 'da-da', I'm just going to have to tell her about Germaine Greer from an early age.

WE HAVE BOUGHT A NEW HOUSE!

Two things happened to make us do this.

We live on a main road in Surbiton. For some reason, the pollution seems worse than ever. I know it just creeps up every year and everyone puts their head in the sand but I think my sense of smell is still heightened and the fumes smell so strong to me.

To demonstrate how good my sense of smell is, I knew my postman had egg for his breakfast. I asked him outright: 'Did you have egg for your breakfast?'

'Yes,' he said, 'at the weekend.'

See, that's how good it is!

And so I can really smell the pollution and it's making me uneasy. I've stopped opening the windows at the front of the house. The diesel fumes are so strong and the sad thing is that I can, for the first time, smell them in the house. I look at my darling baby and I look at the vans and lorries and all the buses standing in traffic outside of our house and I think what a shame her first, formative years are being spent breathing it all in.

I mentioned it to Jon: 'Wouldn't it be amazing to be surrounded by trees and not main roads?' He agreed and next thing we were looking on Rightmove. I bloody love Rightmove. I'm addicted to it; any chance I have I'm on there, looking up places where we're never actually going to move to, like Bridlington or Dundee, just to see what we could have. Though I've noticed I look at Rightmove a lot more when the house is a mess, which made me realize I'm not actually looking at property, I'm addicted to looking at tidy houses!

This time though I wanted a tidy house and I wanted to leave Surbiton.

I'm not sure how but I found Hebden Bridge on Rightmove. We saw a house on there that had a tree-lined drive and greenery out of every window. I could taste the air almost; it was sweet and it was cold because it's in a valley near the Pennines. I didn't actually know at the time that the area was home to most of the UK's asbestos mills but luckily that seems to have died down a bit now and the people look happy on the local tourist board site. Yes, it's probably still in the soil a bit but they do have a lovely organic food shop in the centre so I expect that cancels it all out.

We went to view the house. It wasn't right for us. We just had that feeling. Weird, isn't it, that feeling you get when you step into the house? 'Am I comfortable having a poo in this house?' I think is basically the gist of it.

The next house we viewed, one village over, needed a bit of work but there was something special about it. It was like meeting a potential lover and just knowing that whatever happened, this person would be in your life for a long time. Like me and Jon. In a world full of confusing things, we had been brought together, we just knew it. Fate.

It's a detached 1930s house that, although loved, has been neglected in a lot of areas. The big selling point is the garden, which has been cherished. It has a large, manicured lawn surrounded by huge, and I mean HUGE, evergreens, and all this for the same price as your small two-bed semi-detached house in Surbiton. Plus, something feels comforting about the house; it has a character of its own. We knew instantly that this was where we should be bringing up our daughter. I also sensed a spirit on the stairs but I think she liked us. Jon pretended I was mad but I could tell I'd spooked him bit.

BUBBLE WRAP

The house sale has been completed. I'm delighted in a way but sad to be leaving London. London can wait, though. I want that fresh air in Elsie's lungs and I want her to play in fields. Oh, and I've left out a massive part of living back Up North – we want to be closer to our families!

A very large Amazon parcel arrived this morning. I opened it and inside was just loads and loads of bubble wrap. I showed it to Jon and we were both really angry. No wonder climate change is so bad! I instantly took to Twitter to share my annoyance, I got Jon to take a picture of it and I started looking up the address to write to Amazon customer services.

And then I remembered I'd ordered bubble wrap. For packing. Jon gave me a sympathetic look. It does show how far I've come, though. When I moved down to London I used my clothes to pack the breakables, which were only a couple of trinkets. I moved to London with four bin liners on the train. I'm now moving from London with about 12 bin liners, a house of furniture, a husband, a 9-month-old baby and 10 tins of custard.

PART FOUR

WHAT IS THAT MAGICAL BEAUTY TREATMENT THEY CALL SLEEP?

OUR HOUSE

We are finally in our new house in Mytholmroyd, West Yorkshire. It is March and Elsie is ten months old. The blossom is out on the trees and the hedges are full of nesting birds. I can see fields and hills and sheep. We held our baby up to the window to see a robin the other day and the biggest rainbow appeared in the sky.

We had a few weeks of bliss together as a family and then it was time for Jon to get back on the road and do the first leg of his tour now that all his warm-up shows were done. Being on my own with our baby suddenly feels very different and I also feel the weight of living somewhere that seems very remote compared to Surrey. I've started to realize that we are nearer to our loved ones who live a couple of hours away but also not near enough. I hope we've made the right choice.

But yesterday something fantastic happened. I met our neighbours, Emma, Damion and their teenage son, Thomas. Emma and Damion are sort of semi-retired. They've worked hard and saved but I don't think they're in their fifties yet. They both work part-time for the council. Thomas is a musical prodigy and he boards at a prestigious music college. Emma has been out weeding her rockery a lot and I think it has taken her a month to do one patch but today we really all hit it off. I stopped a lot longer to chat and I realized what a great sense of humour they all have; we just clicked. I think me and Jon might be a bit of an enigma to them, coming up to this sleepy West Yorkshire village with our funny London ways.

I told Damion I was having nachos for tea and he couldn't believe it.

'Warm crisps?' he said.

'Yes, with guacamole,' I replied.

He tried to make the word with his lips but gave up and laughed at me for having such a weird-sounding condiment. I just couldn't wait to see them again the next day.

The next day Emma was still weeding her rockery, I walked past with Elsie in her pram and she was sucking on some big juicy raisins. Emma commented on them.

'I've never had a raisin.'

'You've never had a raisin?' I couldn't believe it.

'No, I've just never fancied one.'

Wow, wow, it actually seems quite profound. It stopped me in my tracks. What a great family! Emma told me that if I needed anything to come to them and how pleased they were that we were neighbours. People like that leave a warm glow in my belly, they are worth holding on to.

POEMS

So much stuff is still in boxes. I can't find my hairbrush and Elsie still isn't sleeping a lot at night. To pass the time, I've been writing poetry. I'm thinking about writing a book of poems about mothering.

I'm going to call it *If My Eyes Were Carrier Bags*.

I've written a few already.

☞ IF MY EYES WERE ☜
CARRIER BAGS

If my eye bags were carrier bags people would say to
*   me, 'Your handle on your bag is gonna snap*
*   love,' or*
'That looks heavy!'
Or my mum would say, 'You need a bag for life, your
*   bags are drooping, I've got one with unicorns*

you can have. You fold it up and put it in
another little bag. What you need to do is leave
it next to your front door and then you won't
forget to take it with you.'
If my eye bags were a fruit they'd be bruised grapes.
Can you bruise grapes? I'm too tired to care,
I am bruised fruit,
I am a heavy bag,
I am a first-time mum.

———

☞ FLAKY PASTRY ☜

What are you looking at?
Yes, I'm eating a cheese and onion pie with one hand
while I hold my baby on the bus with the other
hand.
Yes, I know I've got it all over my top, it's in my hair,
it's on my face. I can feel it.
My child has finally fallen asleep, she's had tummy
trouble.
I haven't eaten all day, I breastfeed, I get hungry
like a docker, I can eat as much as a six-foot-
two scaffolder, I like the same food as sumo
wrestlers.
I need calories and sugar,
I need a lot of sugar,

Sugar is life, it keeps me going. Don't judge me,
I can drink custard all day and not put weight on.
Don't you dare walk over to me to tell me my pasty
 is all over the place, I'll make a scoop with my
 top and take it with me, it will float out of me
 into the air, like fairy dust but if fairies were all
 sponsored by Greggs,
Here you come, go on, you dare say anything to me,
 you, you man, you man who has no idea…
 What's that? What did you just say to me?
Is the next stop Halifax, yes it is, sorry, yep, bye take
 care, aw, thanks (he said the baby was cute.)
I look down at my baby, her face is covered in bits of
 flaky pastry, so I lick it off her forehead DON'T
 JUDGE ME!!!!

I've re-read my poetry and I've come to realize that if Philip Larkin had had kids then his poetry would also be a bit like this.

A GOOD OMEN

Today I called Emma to ask if she wanted anything from the shop. She sounded relaxed so I asked if she'd just had a nap. 'No,' she said, 'I'm just laid on our Thomas's bed stroking his gun.'

I have decided not to tell Jon about this phone conversation. They're such a wonderful family he might take it the wrong way!

Later in the day, Emma popped over to check I was alright as she knew Jon was away. She caught me off guard. The house was a tip as I've been struggling to keep up with everything you need to keep up with and I was a bit weepy. I burst out crying and Emma hugged me and told me everything was going to be okay. She said she was going to bring over a pork dinner for me. I told her I'm vegan. She nodded and went back for it. It was left on the back porch with a pudding in a dish and a little jug of custard. It was like an omen. I might not be close enough to my friends and family and normal civilization but I have the best neighbours.

THINGS I HAVE DONE BECAUSE I'M TIRED AT THE NEW HOUSE

1   My dear new neighbour Helen has a beautiful immaculate house and a chicken. It's a lovely chicken called Brenda. It was Helen's fiftieth birthday recently and I

addressed the card to Brenda. But that's not even the bad bit. I went to Helen's house for her party lunch and I called her Brenda for the entire time I was there.

2 Yesterday I took my dear baby to the park. It was 2pm on a Wednesday but I put her in a delightful little tartan outfit with a matching headband that she removed before we'd left the house. I went to get a cup of tea from the café and was stopped by a lady I'd worked with on the radio. She said, 'Oh Lucy, she's gorgeous, what's her name?'

I paused. My heart started to beat faster.

'I can't remember,' I said. 'Errrmm.'

I look at my cherub-faced child, hoping something would remind me.

'It begins with E.'

She laughed and then looked horrified when she realized I was serious.

I forgot my child's name. The shame. She gave me that sympathetic face – you know the one I mean.

3 I've found it helps me get off to sleep if I read. I don't think I'm the first person to realize this but it really works, despite the fact I am still getting woken up twice a night for a feed that Elsie no longer needs.

I'm reading a book about feminism. It's made me think a lot about this notion of 'everyday sexism'. I am under no illusion that my anger towards sexism is being fuelled by a year of not enough sleep. I'm very angry. I'm very tired. I'm mad that women are treated like objects.

There is a lot of building work happening at the bottom of our street. Over the last few weeks, every time I've walked to the shops, one of the builders has shouted 'Cheer up love' or 'Give us a smile'. I said to myself this morning if he does it again I'm going to say something to him, like Emmeline Pankhurst.

I went past him today, and he shouted 'Aww, give us a smile, pet!'

I thought, right, I'm not having that. I shouted back: 'EXCUSE ME, I LIVE IN A SEMI-DETACHED HOUSE.'

On my return from the shop I passed him again and he said nothing to me.

I had won!

BABY GROUPS

I really enjoy going to playgroups with my baby. I've been 'playgroup hopping' to find the one that suits us, there are so many. We went to a Steiner one, that was WEIRD. It was like being in a Netflix documentary about a cult. I knew it was odd when I walked in and there were just a few wooden toys and everyone was quiet. Even Elsie thought it was weird. Everyone was in tie-dye and, don't get me wrong, I'm a raving bad vegan, but these guys had spent years chained to trees. They were all very friendly and we sat around for a snack, which was carrots and apples, but, before we did, the babies had to follow a ritual of washing their hands in an urn while we chanted a song and they all sang it like ghosts.

My daughter gave me a look as if to say, 'What are you playing at? Get me out of here!' So we left. It wasn't hard to find our shoes as not many had turned up in them.

I instantly felt the need to get a McDonalds and buy a DFS sofa just to level out the hippy vibes. I'm sure for us to save the planet we all should be acting like that but, well, my animalistic brain told me to run.

The second playgroup made me feel better about myself, but too much. I felt superior, and I'm sure a lot of people would think that's the perfect place to be in to make friends, but superior in the way that I'd managed to have a flannel wash before we went and I didn't swear around the children. I went for a few weeks until I couldn't handle that people weren't brushing their hair. I don't brush my hair on week days but I like to be the only one. Our pram is covered in food and mud and gosh knows what else and I sometimes went with my PJs on underneath my jogging bottoms, but at least I had that inner voice telling me I should be making more of an effort. This led to my outer voice telling the organizer that she should be sanitizing the toys more. Once you've told the leader of a playgroup that the toys are dirty that's generally the 'goodbye Susan' moment. We didn't go back. Never explain, always complain – I think that's the mantra for playgroups?

I found another playgroup, this time under the watchful, cleansing eyes of God, at a church. It was run by women who I'm sure liked children when they first started. They of course wanted us all to join the church in return for their playgroup efforts but as they were Church of England, they were too polite to tell us that. We did have to sing songs about God halfway through, which they apologized for and afterwards they did a little buffet to make up for it. I like God, I like religion and I love songs about him having the whole world in his hands and Elsie likes cream crackers so we were winning.

The first time we attended, I was caught off guard as all the other mothers had Land Rovers and smelled of Daz. There was an air of 'togetherness'. Some had curled their hair; the children looked immaculate and had matching accessories. It seemed like a lot of thought and preparation had been put in but I had enough of a balanced humble upbringing to know this was down to two things: money and time.

I heard one of the Land Rover mums slagging off the other playgroup. She'd only been once and I'd been four times, and I was half-heartedly invited to a beer garden afterwards, so I was allowed to slag it off. I had a pang of wanting to protect the other mothers at the rough playgroup but I kept quiet. I hated myself for this but I needed to make friends. This is where I belonged. It had soap in the toilet and parents used wet wipes.

The problem was, I didn't look like I fitted in, which I know deep down is because I had become lazy due to tiredness. I could tell that no one in this room was getting the sort of broken sleep that I was getting but still, I had to really up my game, to prove to them that I was not just as good as them, I was better than them because my husband was on television.

It was very cliquey, everyone knew each other, but very soon they'd realize who my husband is and then they'd be nice. I've had that loads and it sucks and is great in equal measure. It happens a lot when we go for tea or lunch at a pub or café. When we go together, we get waited on hand and foot and then I'll go back on another day, this time without Jon, thinking it's such a lovely place, and I'll get treated differently because they've forgotten me. They're just a bit ruder, just a bit more offhand…like they are to everyone else.

The next week I had a plan.

First, I washed all our clothes with loads and loads of fabric softener. I use eco stuff normally that doesn't have any fragrance because I've lived in north London, but for this mission I needed full-strength Lenor so I could smell like them, like middle-class northerners.

Then I went to bed the night before the playgroup at the same time as my child: 7.30 pm. Yes, she still woke three times in the night but I had at least been in bed ten hours.

I set my alarm early so I could wash and blow dry my hair

before she awoke. I had breakfast, which was three Jaffa cakes and some poppadoms from an Indian takeaway. I applied my make-up and, when Elsie woke up, I played with her, gave her lots of cuddles and read to her. Sadly Peppa Pig entertained her while I set about cleaning the pram and making my nappy bag look like it had nappies in it but I was feeling superior. I chose a long jumper dress, like the other mums at the playgroup, and I curled just the front bit of my hair, because one of the other mums had done this last time I went.

I knew that was ten minutes that I could be spending with my baby, helping her develop a personality. But I also knew at this moment that their opinion of me counted more than my child, my husband and our mortgage even. So…

The next thing I need to mention is although I want approval from the 'Laura Ashley Mums', I also want approval from the type of people I went to uni with. Not my actual friends from uni – they're wonderful, accepting people who really know me well. I mean the ones who didn't become my friends. I want to do things that I know they'd be accepting of, even though I'll never see them again. That's why I bought my child a mud kitchen. If you don't know what it is, a mud kitchen is an outdoor set-up that encourages your child to pretend to cook with mud and it's what you buy when you have bought them everything else they need and still need to fill a hole in your own soul with online purchases. It is also backed up by the Scandinavian idea that if your child plays with mud and has that connection with nature they won't get depressed when they're older. So basically my child will be happy for the rest of her life because she has a mud kitchen. It has also taught her to explore with her hands – she's not scared of getting dirty.

We walked in to the playgroup, both of us looking a million dollars. We totally could have been on the front cover of an industry magazine for designer prams, in my opinion. As soon as we got inside, we headed over to the messy corner, which was a table full of sensory things: Play-Doh, glue, coloured water, slime, etc. As we approached, almost in slow motion a child was sick onto the table. Everyone rushed around trying to help and I nearly tripped over another child, so had to divert slightly left of the sick on the table. Meanwhile, the mother whose child had been sick diverted to the right to fetch her handbag, thereby giving my child clear access to the sick. She picked it up, letting it ooze through her hands, dropping on her cleaned and ironed top. The other mums gasped, like she was a cannibal about to eat human flesh. I knew exactly what was going to happen.

'NOOO! Don't, don't…liiiick iiiiit!'

'Custard!' my daughter exclaimed.

Oh gosh, what have I done to her?!

THE OTHER BUNNY GIRL

Last night was a tough one: three wake ups and then she wanted to get up at 5.45am. I tried to get her to go back to sleep but it didn't work. It's a different type of tiredness when you've not slept well and you wake up before 6am. My brain goes a bit wappy. This is the time though, while watching *Bing* on TV, that I have my mad ideas. My idea today was that I felt like doing something out of the ordinary. I looked up 'bunny costumes' on the internet. Not those supposedly sexy bunny outfits, which, I must add, I don't find sexy. (I've never understood those bunny girls. They look really pretty and polished with white shiny teeth and flawless make-up and then they turn around and they've got an animal's tail attached to them.) No, I've been looking for full bunny suits with a big bunny heads too. I'd like a huge one, maybe with a bow tie that's got holes for my eyes or something. I don't know how I'd breathe in it, though. I like the idea of putting on a costume and being invisible. I'd love to go out dressed as a Big Bunny and make people smile, in parks or at festivals. Or maybe in the future

I'll do the school run wearing it. Perhaps I could be a lollipop bunny and help children across the roads.

There's a lady in Hull who for nearly all my life has dressed up as a bee and stood in Hull city centre collecting money for charity. Every Saturday. She might be the sweetest lady ever or maybe she just killed a few people and felt bad about it and wanted a way to make amends.

If I went into the park dressed like a bunny I think the teenagers with badly rolled spliffs would chase after me but then eventually I'd be welcomed and accepted in the town. People would wait for me to come along.

It got to 8.45am so I called my mum about the idea I had. She said in a very concerned voice, 'Have you told Jon?'

'I'm not saying I'm going to have an affair, I just thought it might bring a little joy to people.'

Mum replied, 'I think you're very odd and I'm worried about you.' Then she paused and said, 'Neil knew a woman who had a one-eyed bunny; it bit her nose off so her husband strangled it.'

I didn't know what to say to that so I didn't say anything.

Mum followed it up with, 'I've posted Elsie a Roman coin. I found it down a well.'

I realized that my bunny idea was daft. Instead I searched for a black-out blind – maybe that'll stop the early wake up time and we all get more sleep.

ISN'T SHE LOVELY

I was having one of those sorts of days where you feel a bit sorry yourself, like you're missing out on something, somewhere. I think I'm missing working. I feel like I only own clothes that smell of baby sick. I really miss feeling like a person in the world, if that makes sense – moving about, carrying a handbag, that sort of thing.

Then Jon shouted to me to come downstairs. Elsie was fingerpainting at the kitchen table and Jon asked her to repeat something.

'My mummy,' she said in this little croaky voice.

I picked her up and span her around. We put on 'Isn't She Lovely', one of Elsie's faves, and we danced, her head on my chest. I could feel her little heart against mine, like the little bird.

'How are you feeling now?' Jon asked.

'I'm going to be fine, I just need to get pissed with my mates, I think.'

'We need to stop swearing in front of her now she's talking.'

'Oh shit, sorry.'

'You need to stop breastfeeding, you know, Lucy,' Jon said in a serious tone. 'You can have your life back then.'

He's right.

How on earth do you just stop breastfeeding, though? We both love it, we love the closeness, it's nectar. Elsie makes little noises of pure happiness and delight while she feeds. Can I really stop breastfeeding?

STAYING WITH MY MUM

I went to stay one night with my mum, to see how our nearly one-year-old would cope without me. I can manage to express enough milk for one night now too, though Elsie doesn't need it anymore – it's not food, she's loving solids, it purely medicinal now. It feels like the way someone has a hot toddy before bed. (What I want to say is it's like how someone has a spliff before bed because it does knock her out, but that seems a bit inappropriate in a book about child-rearing!)

My mum loved that I needed to come and stay with her. I've never really done that before so she was getting her baby back in a way, just for one night. Though I think she could sense that I wasn't myself – it wasn't just about getting a bit of a respite.

I collapsed on her sofa and told her that I thought I was a shit mum and I didn't really know what I was doing. (Apart from the mud kitchen.)

My mum said, 'It'll come.' Just like that: 'It'll come.'

Sometimes she can really seem like a fountain of knowledge, with life and people. Such wise words. I believed her.

I went upstairs. She'd made the spare room really lovely for me – she'd put the lamp on, which I thought was a sweet touch, to create ambience and because the main light doesn't work. There was a lit candle on the bedside table, clean bedding and a tiger-skin blanket draped over a chair with a love heart cushion on it. An out-of-date chocolate was on my bed and in the window there was a cardboard cut-out of Elvis Presley, and a monkey hung off the curtain rail.

I laid on the bed and exhaled deeply. I felt my shoulders relaxing; tonight I would sleep like a baby. My mum shouted to me from the bottom of the stairs.

'DO YOU WANT TO USE MY VAGISIL? IT'S FOR WOMEN UP TO THE AGE OF 55.'

The next day was glorious. I got up late and watched *Homes Under the Hammer* in my mum's dressing gown while she kept coming through from the kitchen to bring me breakfast-related snacks.

Our conversation when I was about to leave went like this:

MUM:

> *Do you want some Mini Cheddars for the train?*

ME:

> *No thanks.*

MUM:

> *How about two tiny satsumas in kitchen roll?*

ME:

> *I'm alright.*

MUM:

> *Do you want some plum tomatoes and a packet of crackers?*

ME:

> *No.*

MUM:

> *Okay, bye.*

My mum looked like she was leaving me to go back into the kitchen but really she was seeing what else she could give me. She rushed back.

MUM:

> *Two Dairylea triangles?*

ME:

> *Okay then, but I don't eat dairy, they rip the calves away from the mother and fill them with antibiotics.*

MUM:

> *Aw, you love your cheese triangles, don't you?*

ME:

Yeah…

MUM:

When you go home, try not to be such a middle-class parent, that's not how you were brought up.

A mother's love.

THE VISITOR

Elsie is 11 months old – 11 months! She's hoovering up all her meals and growing so quickly. She likes Yorkshire pudding the best. I hide bits of veg inside them and she spits out the veg and says 'Heck!' like a proper northern lass. She's strong too, with big fists and expressive eyes – no hair yet, though, so basically she looks like a regular in some of the pubs I've worked in. She can't half crawl fast too, and she pulls herself up and knocks over everything at head height. Again, like some of the regulars I've served in pubs.

The days are long and active but the weeks zoom by and I love it but I also still haven't had a proper night's sleep for nearly a year. I know I bang on about it but it's the main obstacle in my otherwise quite serene life. I still have bags under my eyes that are like half-moons. If I was a stargazer I might like to look at my eye bags in the mirror and marvel at their lunar colours. What is really mad is that because I'm still breastfeeding I'm not drinking coffee. I read on the internet that you can have one cup but I'm worried the caffeine would make my soon-to-be toddler stay awake even more. Besides, I still like drinking custard for a natural high.

I'll be honest, I have actually noticed a lot of benefits from not drinking coffee. I know it gives you an instant hit but you do crash again. Whereas when you don't drink it your whole day is like a slow-motion crash but there is a point a bit later on when you have a burst of energy. This might be when I decide to do something crazy, like put on make-up to go to the newsagents.

It's not just because of the broken sleep at night that I'm tired, it's also still the napping situation. Elsie still wants to sleep in the pram while it's moving. I suppose she feels safe with the motion of it and me sweating next to her. I'm longing to be able to put her down in her cot and clean up for an hour or have a nap myself. Or look at Facebook, of course. Facebook is the new napping.

I've noticed a lot of older people are joining Facebook and the younger ones are going on TikTok. A similar thing happened to Saturday nights in Hull. All the old folks started to drink in the old town pubs and the young people started going out on a Thursday instead. They say the sad thing about getting older is realizing that youth is wasted on the young. I think the sad thing about getting older is realizing young people don't want to hang around with you.

But LOOK here. I am really skirting around a certain subject. I'm trying to create a build-up to it, give you some sort of perspective in the hope that you won't judge me. What I've done today is the most middle-class thing I've ever done. In fact, it's not just middle class, it's London middle class. It's not even just London middle class, it's for a certain type of twat. And I am that twat. No, I am, BUT I'm a twat who doesn't live near family, or not close enough, so…I'm going to just spit it out.

I hired a sleep trainer.

Oh gosh, I can't even bear to see it written down. I'm embarrassed about my smugness. I feel like when you go jogging past two men eating burgers in a white van. I also feel terrible, terrible guilt. On the one hand, it feels like something a lot of people would like to do and yet also something that you would have to be careful about how you told even your closest friends. I just wasn't brought up like this. Well, no one was, it's a new thing, maybe American. And it's because I married someone off the telly.

I was brought up to go to car boot sales and say 'Ooh, very posh' when someone has feta cheese. Our family are very creative but we like pub meals that are two for the price of one and taking spare change to play on the amusements at the seaside. I was brought up to hold my granny's fag while she played bingo but I also visited a lot of editing studios in central London with my dad who worked in post-production, so, you know, I've got range! But even so, people like me, WE DO NOT HIRE SLEEP TRAINERS!

The thing is, Elsie has been particularly upset and grumpy for the last two days. It's been really hard to settle her and the purpose of a sleep trainer is to promote good sleeping habits. They say they can help set up a napping routine and hopefully help your baby sleep through the night. This is what they claim. I didn't ask how they do it and also I didn't ask if there was a guarantee. I just booked us in. It's a London-based company so I was very surprised that the trainer was prepared to come up to West Yorkshire.

Let's see how it goes!

SAFFRON

I've just had the most bizarre two days of my life and I don't say that lightly.

Jon went away and the sleep trainer arrived. She seemed on edge and not, I'll be honest, that interested in my baby. She was hungry and asked if she could cook a meal. She put on a housecoat and made herself at home. I did try to change the subject away from her divorce and wanting to set up a saffron farm in Nottinghamshire. I wasn't being rude but I didn't know her that well yet and I really wanted some help with getting my baby to sleep. I probed her on her knowledge of all things baby-related and explained how Elsie hadn't settled at all the last couple of nights but this woman seemed to just want to talk about herself. I kept thinking back to the very professional, eloquent lady on the phone from the agency – she sounded like she'd attended a very good university, surely she wouldn't have sent me a nutter?

'This curry I'm making is for all of us. I'm worried you're eating too much processed crap. When I stay with people, I take care of the mother first, you see.'

'You're staying over, are you? Oh...'

'Well, you live in the middle of nowhere. If you were in London I could go home. Well, not at the moment as I don't actually have a home right now but, as I say, the farm in Nottingham, I've manifested it so it is going to happen. There's money in saffron, you know.'

'I've heard that.'

'Who have you heard it from?'

'I don't know, my grandad maybe. I can't remember.'

'Not someone with a farm, then?'

'No, he's just got a bungalow.'

'You need a sweet potato and some fresh herbs. Can you go and get some?

'Yeah, no problem!'

And so I went. I packed Elsie up in her pram, both of us exhausted, and went to get a woman I'd only just met, who I'd paid to come and live with me accidently on purpose when she could have stayed in a Premier Inn, a sweet potato. I don't understand.

I can get so fiery with some people, I can really blow and give some people what for. I don't suffer fools but when someone walks into your house, puts on a housecoat and tells you to go get a sweet potato, well, you do it.

I was dreading going back. I rang Jon – who, by the way, had told me it was a ridiculous idea to hire a sleep trainer.

'How's it going?' he asked.

'Oh brilliant, she's really good. I made the right choice.'

'Where are you?' he said.

'Just in Co-op getting a sweet potato.'

I got back and as we ate, she told me her life story. Sometimes she'd ask me questions but she wasn't really listening when I replied. I then said I needed to put my baby to bed, trying to remind her why she was actually here. I.e. 'WHEN ARE YOU GOING TO HELP ME?'

While I breastfed Elsie, the trainer got in her pyjamas that were very thick and fluffy, and maybe a bit too warm to sleep in, so I think this was actually more like her second indoor outfit, or maybe she thought the north was very, very cold. Who knows? It threw me, though. It had bears on and was a bit like a toddler's onesie. I suppose I just didn't think someone who wanted a saffron farm would wear something like that.

The room I put her in was next to Elsie's. I could see her shadow on the corridor wall as she'd left her door open, of course. She was doing some exercises. Before we came upstairs I did manage to squeeze in that it was difficult putting Elsie down when she wasn't fully asleep but that seemed to be what everyone was banging on about to do. If you breastfeed to sleep and put them in their cot they will wake up when they realize you're not there, so you need to set them down when they're sleepy but not totally asleep so they can get to sleep by themselves.

Have you ever tried to stop breastfeeding a baby at the point where they're sleepy but not fully asleep? It takes place in a nanosecond, undetectable by the naked eye. Basically, it would be easier to ask the baby to go out and get a buy-to-let mortgage! It's impossible. But of course Lady Saffron agreed I needed to do it. So I laid Elsie down in her cot. She woke up and stared at me. She wasn't sleepy enough. I raised my voice a bit to tell the trainer, who was in the next room, that Elsie was down in her cot and then… She CRAWLED IN. She CRAWLED on her hands and knees in a fluffy bear onesie.

'What are you doing?' I asked.

'It's important they don't see me or know I'm here; it could disturb them.'

I was already thinking about the review I would give on the website: '*After sending me to search for sweet potato in the small village of Mytholmroyd, the trainer talked about saffron, did lunges in a bear onesie and crawled on her hands and knees around the nursery.*'

The trainer looked at my baby and said, 'She's in pain, that wriggling around she's doing, look.'

'She does that a lot,' I said.

'Well, it's not normal. She's trying to get to sleep and she can't because she's in pain. You need to pick her up and breastfeed her to sleep, if that's what she needs, if it's helping her. We'll get to the bottom of this tomorrow.'

Can you imagine? I cried like a baby. In an instant I was so glad she was here.

The next day was hard. The trainer went through all of my cupboards and made me write a diary. She kept reminding me how good it was that we still had her stew left. We tried to work out what it was that was causing Elsie's pain. We went through the birth and we then talked about dairy but I explained I was a neurotic woman with a BA honours degree in drama so of course I'd tried to cut out dairy but it hadn't made a difference.

Then we heard it. We heard the almighty rumble, the biggest fart a baby could ever make – wow, the bass on it.

'Oh, there you go then, problem solved,' the trainer said.

I exhaled and sat down. I looked over and Elsie smiled with relief and wonderment; it was one of the loudest farts I'd ever heard. Sorted it, then. It was trapped wind. I felt everything in my body relax. Oh gosh, then I remembered…

'Are you here for two nights?' I asked quickly.

'Yeah,' she said. 'So let me tell you about saffron.'

The second day and night were like being the last people at Glastonbury Festival. She did all the cooking again but the house was a state as I didn't feel I could clean my kitchen, or cook in it or stand in it, as it was very much her domain. She just kept saying, 'I don't know where anything goes.' I now have a rule that if someone is cooking or cleaning in your kitchen and they don't know where anything goes then they shouldn't be doing it.

Instead, I kept a watchful eye on my child. Elsie was fine, she just wanted the lady to leave too. And finally she did. I breathed out fully for the first time in 48 hours. My daughter gave me a sympathetic look. 'I'll write that experience in a book one day,' it said.

Now, here's the thing: my child slept the whole way through that night!

Can you believe it? It was the first ever time with no waking up. I woke up four times of course. On the fourth time I went to check she was still breathing I realized the stupidity of it. After all, she wasn't dead the other times. I persuaded myself to go back to bed and from then on I had a good night's sleep!

What had happened, then? Was it fluke? Was my daughter so scared by the whole experience that she thought she'd better get some shut eye in case the lady came back again? Had she actually had trapped wind for a year and it was now starting to release? Or was that woman actually Jesus?

I had dismissed her and actually she was a miracle worker. And, like an intense Mary Poppins, she's now flown to another family, where I imagine she is wrecking their house, crawling around their bedroom in thick PJs, making them go in search of sweet potatoes and talking about saffron too much – BUT getting their kids to sleep. I just keep wondering, will my daughter sleep right through tomorrow night?

THE NEXT NIGHT

No, she didn't. She woke up twice. Well, actually, she woke up three times but the third time as I reached her door she couldn't be arsed to carry on shouting at me and went back to sleep. I had a wee and went back to bed.

BATHTIME

Elsie's talking is amazing! It's really coming on leaps and bounds now she's 11 months. But a little knowledge is a dangerous thing.

I went to take her out of the bath; she pulled away. I tried again; she shouted at me to get off. I asked nicely, still she resisted. I explained in a calm, firm voice that the bath water was now getting cold, she'd played enough so would she kindly get out. Again she ignored me. I gave her a five-minute warning. She started to shiver. I tried to scoop her up again; she wriggled out.

'Will you get out now please?'

'No,' she said.

'I need you to get out of the bath, you're getting cold.'

'No.'

And then it happened, I really lost my temper with her for the first time ever. It was still pretty mild but I had until that moment never told her off. I'd not really needed to but here I was, a bit baffled about what to do. Then my mum took over me, and her mum before her, and all of the Hull women that had been in my life, all the eighties upbringing…

'WELL, FATHER CHRISTMAS IS WATCHING, EVEN THOUGH IT'S SUMMER AND ALL YOU'LL GET IN YOUR SACK IS TWO LUMPS OF COAL AND A TANGERINE.'

Still nothing.

'Will you get out now?'

'No,' she said.

'It'll get wrapped around your ribcage and rot your insides.'

Still nothing

'Will you get out now?'

'Nope,' she said again.

'THERE ARE CHILDREN IN AFRICA DYING! Will you get out now?'

'No.'

'Do you want an olive?'

'Yes,' she said and lifted up her arms for me to get her out.

There was no going back now.

BIRTHDAY NUMBER ONE

We have done it, we have raised a one-year-old! A year. A FULL YEAR! And yesterday we celebrated.

I unintentionally invited half of the region of Calderdale to our house for Elsie's birthday. When I said to people, 'We're having a party, come along, bring your family,' I didn't think that a LOT of people would bring ALL of their family. I've just been desperate for us to feel like part of the community. I just love stopping and chatting to people in the street. So, yesterday I had the street(s) in our house.

On a positive note, as I said to Jon, who didn't know about the open invitations, what it does show is that people are very friendly up here. I invited all the neighbours and all the workmen who had worked on our house and they brought their extended families – one of our builders brought four generations of his family. You don't get that in Surrey much!

I also invited all my family, all Jon's family and all my friends and his friends. It was raining so we had to stay inside. Can you imagine, a big garden like we've got and everyone had to stay inside? I also bought a 12-foot blow-up flamingo. My dad blew it up in the living room but really struggled to get out of the room. So the living room was sort of out of bounds. That's how big this flamingo was.

I went with a flamingo theme throughout as I'd seen it on Instagram. I had flamingo everything. I even had the bust of a flamingo head hung up, like they do with stags. I think that a flamingo theme looks very colourful but also looks like a breakdown.

The house was so crowded, Elsie didn't like it, so she refused to come downstairs. The kids ran around the garden in the rain and then brought all the mud in and I never got to speak to my grandad – he was unable to move in a tightly packed out corner, but I managed to crawl under a table to get to him and give him the last sausage roll.

I coaxed Elsie down after a while by making a trail of fizzy cola bottles down the stairs. We all sang 'Happy Birthday' to her and it sounded like a loud amateur choir – we could have filled a football stadium. Elsie cried. Actually, she wailed and clung on to me like a scared koala and I knew in that moment that I had created a fear of parties and singing. After I calmed her down, she looked up to see a giant flamingo head looking down at her and she cried again, so we took her back upstairs and she watched *Frozen* with her grannies instead.

Jon kept asking, 'Why are there so many people here?' In the end I had to keep out of his way. Luckily he went to pick up my aunt Barbara and there was a bad traffic jam and then she needed to stop for a wee quite a few times so he missed a lot of the party, which he was glad of, though it did create a bit of atmosphere as everyone saw him take off in his electric car and not return for ages.

Next year, I will make it a small affair!

EXPRESS YOURSELF

The next morning I was trying to clean up after the party and our little terror seemed a bit put out by all the commotion. She was wanting to latch on for a feed every five minutes. I think it was sort of for attention. I was becoming a bit flustered by it. So I did it: I said 'NO'.

I refused, but I felt like I was denying her what was rightfully hers. Jon came through and I looked at him and said, 'That's it, we have to stop.' He agreed and was pleased; our daughter was not. I don't think for one minute this was the right way to kickstart the weaning process and I'll be totally honest, it felt a bit traumatic as she was so upset. I can see why in the natural parenting books they tell you to just wait until they want to stop by themselves but I had been trying from about nine months to slowly wean her off and nothing has worked. Now I needed to do it. For me. To stop breastfeeding and have a glass of wine to celebrate…This is why I felt so bad.

Then I had an idea. I fetched her a bag of chocolate buttons instead and amazingly she was really, really happy with the swap.

Half an hour later, she wanted another breastfeed. Just because it's become like an activity, like the way you have a swig of water in a tennis match. Again I offered her a chocolate button and she was delighted.

Then came the big one, the bit I'd been dreading all day: the feed before bed. Before her bath, I told her I wouldn't be able to feed her any more milk and that it was just for babies but she could have a button. She thought about it and agreed and Jon put her to bed, no problem, no fuss. Wow, just like that.

I went into the kitchen and cried. I cried because it was all ending and cried because it felt like a new beginning. Nowhere, in none of the books I'd read or on any of the websites, did it tell me about this or about how I'd feel or even offer guidance for the right way to do it all. There's so much information about starting to breastfeed, but how about stopping?

My boobs filled up with milk and I expressed into the sink. Well…that's not totally true. Jon ran himself a bath after he'd put her down and I went to the loo and I started to leak a bit so

I squirted some of it in his bath.

That wasn't all though, I had a little incident the next day.

Jon bought a projector for our spare room so we could watch movies in it. He wanted it professionally installed so he hired an electrician. I'd set Elsie down for her nap and the electrician wasn't in the spare room and his van had gone so I climbed into the bed for a nap – yes, the time is here now when I can nap. We have cracked the secret of napping properly just before she's about to drop them.

I had a wonderful nap, only about half an hour but I felt like a million dollars. I was a bit chilly so I found one of Jon's jackets and put it on. Elsie was still fast asleep so I went downstairs to make a snack. My boobs were killing with the amount of milk in them, like bags of bricks, and so I had to express. I knocked one of my boobs and the milk squirted out, I couldn't believe it. I reached for the nearest thing I could find which was a Peppa Pig bowl, placed it on the coffee table and expressed into it. It was like a jet, honestly – like those water guns you get at theme parks where you have to squirt a target. I could have turned up with good old 'Red' and 'Blue' (their nicknames) and saved myself £2. I was really taken aback by my range and aim so I pushed the Peppa Pig bowl back a bit and, wow! I got it in from about a half metre away. I pushed the bowl back further and I just about reached the bowl and then the electrician walked in.

His face dropped. He had just walked in to see me squirt breast milk into a Peppa Pig bowl from an impressive distance, wearing a man's jacket.

I imagine I had sent him into fight-or-flight mode as he left the room incredibly quickly and shouted back to me as he climbed the stairs: 'I...I...I just went to get some raw plugs, I can't seem to find the pack I had.'

'I'm sorry, I was just expressing, I bet you've seen it all before, haven't you?'

Silence.

'The bra's from Marks & Spencer.'

That was the moment I realized I was turning into my mother.

Jon got home shortly after the electrician left. I nearly jumped on him to tell him what had happened but he stopped me in my tracks.

'Is that a man's jacket you're wearing?'

'Yeah, it's yours.'

'That's not mine.'

I felt in the pocket of the jacket. RAW PLUGS.

'Oh, GOD.'*

---

* Jon – The old Jon would have pointed out that they are not called 'raw plugs' but this book has been a learning process for me and so I will simply allow you to go on calling them what you like, in the name of the farmer and the sun and the mouldy coat.

CRYING, TALKING, SLEEPING, WALKING!

The 12-month mark was a big moment for us. I haven't mentioned that Elsie also learned to walk the day after her party. I did worry if this was because she saw that I was so inept at organizing even a normal child's party and thought she'd better learn to do simple physical tasks herself.

A lot happened then. We realized how much furniture is her head height in our house and how many objects are now reachable. When she's off, she's off! Her favourite thing is to use the coffee table to hold on to and walk around it, knocking off everything she comes into contact with. What I really like is that she looks like she's drunk, like she's been daytime drinking and now needs to use the bar as support as she heads to the toilet.

We also have to do health-and-safety recces everywhere we go. I feel a bit like a bodyguard to someone globally famous – we walk into a café and I have to clock everything, be aware of where the exits and entrances are in case she runs out, scan for dogs that she might want to poke, the flowers and vases on the table and any trip hazards in front of her.

But do you know what? Despite all of this, we've become more relaxed. Mad, isn't it? Because she's also become more robust. I feel out of that danger zone – only in a small way but, well, we've made it this far…

POSTMAN PAT

Goodness, she keeps us busy!

My daughter's speech is too developed for her age. At 16 months, she is correcting the way I speak. It's starting to upset me but I've raised her like this. What is so lovely is that although she speaks very well, she says the word 'work' like me – she draws it out so it sounds slightly Liverpudlian but is very Hull: 'weeerk'.

She doesn't know she does it and I hope it stays.

I read one of her favourite books to her tonight. It's a Postman Pat one and there's a parrot in it called Mickawabber. Elsie softly stroked my cheek and whispered to me, 'Mummy, it's Micawber.' It was a terrible moment for me.

I went downstairs to Jon and said we're over-stimulating her; she's becoming too intelligent too quickly. I said she still has the emotions of a one-year-old, yet her speech and comprehension are far beyond her years and she might struggle to make friends if we don't just ease off. He nearly believed me until he asked what has kickstarted this feeling in me and I explained she corrected me, the way I pronounced Mick-a-wab-ber. Jon laughed, a proper belly laugh. The damage has been done, we have a very intelligent daughter who is actually socially very good, there's no going back and this is going to be the beginning of her realizing that I say stupid things sometimes. God help me.

PART FIVE

TODDLING ALONG

HOME ALONE

Jon went away for two weeks today. When he left, Elsie shut the door and turned to me, with her hands on hips, and said 'Right, I'm in charge now.'

I said, 'I don't think so.' But we both knew she was right.

Like most parents, I spend a lot of time alone with a small human. I love it but it also makes my brain like mush. It's not my *child* that does this, it's the endless repetitive tasks you have to do and the trying to tidy away toys and get out the door with lots of daft things. A trip to the shops needs: nappy, wipes, butt cream, a drink, snacks for the way there and back, a changing mat, hand gel, a check of the weather, a rain hood, maybe suncream and a hat. Is it chilly? Get a scarf. She won't wear gloves so get a blanket. Then there's the precise feeding times and napping times, the cartoons, the sounds the toys make, trying to make sure the house isn't dusty, keeping her clothes clean and her crockery sanitized. It's MENTAL and it's worse if your brain wasn't wired up for anything practical. I remember one of my friends at primary school telling me, quite matter-of-factly and with a level of perception quite beyond her years, that I didn't have any common sense. I've really run with this, to be honest. I've lived my life by it and if I've ever found myself in a situation where I needed to have common sense I've quickly turned the other way. To be fair, it's turned out quite well so far!

It's been a slightly bizarre couple of days without Jon here. I'm wearing his socks a lot and not showering. The child is of course getting my full attention, which is why the house is upside down. I've got time to be at a toddler's beck and call if I follow the simple rule of 'when I get something out I don't put it away'. This rule applies to all rooms of the house and every activity. I'm envious of these mothers you hear about who have three kids and breed dogs and still have a show home.

My main stress is trying to conform to the woman I pretended to be when I met my husband – that is, a domesticated one. Don't get me wrong, I'm not lazy or unhygienic (the current lack of showering notwithstanding, though I do love a strip wash in winter – where you just have a little dab around with a flannel) and I do like tidying up, but for some reason I like to do it in the way a teenager tidies when they've had a secret gatecrashed party at their parents' house and they're coming home an hour earlier than expected.

The reason for all this, for my disorganization – and that's what it is – is because I'm in cloud cuckoo land most of the time. The geography teacher at school was right. He might have had two failed marriages and a crap car but he got me. I am 'away with the fairies' and what's lovely now is that I take my little cherub of a child with me to this day-dream land. Well, we sort of board the same spaceship and then she's on her own little planet.

You see, Elsie is now 20 months old and she seems to be developing so fast I can hardly keep up, let alone write it all down in a diary. She, too, now loves to play in an imaginary land and not notice the utter destruction of 'things' strewn around the place. Will she change? Yes, if I constantly, as soon as she's playing, interrupt her flow and tell her to put it away; if she starts to become anxious when things are untidy because of years of me following her around huffing and puffing. There are different horses for different courses and I stopped trying to pretend I can put my life in order. It's a beautiful life I've got despite people having told me I wouldn't amount to anything if I wasn't organized.

It's a beautiful and messy life. I do get my shit together eventually but it takes a bit longer than most people. My daughter will most likely grow up not knowing where her phone charger and bank card are, but I hope if this is the case she is attracted to a life partner (she might have more than one of course) who can fill in the gaps.

Look at me – when I first set eyes on good old Jon I thought, 'Wow, here's a man who can keep my passport in a safe place.'

OH MY GOD SHE'S TWO YEARS OLD!

We did it, we reached two years old! We've just had the most wonderful party. It consisted of me, the child, her father and the nannas. We had tea and cake, I washed up as I went along and there were no flamingos in sight! And to top it all she didn't mind, she preferred it.

The only sad thing was we went to sing 'Happy Birthday' to

her and she started shaking and crying – bit too soon from the trauma of last year.

All character-building though, isn't it?!

Yesterday I had this burst of energy so I got us both dressed and we headed out. Elsie got caught up in the excitement. We were just going to the town centre but she fed off my energy, I could see, and it was as if we were going to Disneyland. What's so magical about this age is anything can be as fun as Disneyland. Building a den, going on an adventure walk, picking up twigs, baking a cake, making funny faces and also going to Co-op (which was in fact where we were going).

On the way to Co-op, we stopped off at a lovely little delicatessen, which we had last visited a couple of weeks ago, when my child had done a massive poo in her nappy and had a meltdown and I had felt-tip all over my face and didn't know. Today, all that was in the past and we strutted into the shop like new women.

I had my act together and I was wearing a neckerchief that colour-coordinated with my daughter's gilet, if anyone noticed. I'm sure on a subconscious level they did. The gilet was from Joules but because I'm not a total snob I got it off eBay and felt better about myself. I'm not judging those who shop at Joules but you have to ask yourself why you'd buy something at those prices for a child who will leak, splurge, spew and regurgitate on it for most of the day.

The shopkeeper, a nice man who looks as if he likes pies and cheeses and wine a lot, asked us if we'd like to try the olives. This didn't happen last time; we did not look like serious buyers of nibbles last time. We laughed as my daughter seemed to gobble up a couple of olives.

'Sophisticated tastes!' the man said.

'Oh yes!' I said. 'She loved them in Italy.'

Bizarre what lack of sleep does. We have never taken her to Italy, so why was I trying to act all lady of the manor with this very down-to-earth West Yorkshire man? But it was working, I think he thought I had a Range Rover outside and that's all I've ever wanted.

So on we went to the play park. My child goes crazy when we enter the park. No, you don't understand, I mean *crazy*, where she can't breathe and I have to hold her until she's calmed down. The shrillness of her squeal goes through people. Most mums look over and think 'hyperactive', but one mum saw us and laughed, finding it funny, which it is. My child was just too excited to actually play on anything. I calmed her down and got chatting to this lovely mum. Her daughter had a similar spark to mine – you could see it there in the eyes, like she was engaged with the world.

I know as I write this it sounds mean but some kids are just a bit gormless when they're little; you'll know if you have one like that, I'm sure. This mum was also funny; we chatted about all sorts of stuff and not just about having kids – she actually had a life and opinions and she was working again. She was like the Billy Goat Gruff that got to the other side. And she was trendy too, she hadn't gone in for all the frumpy mum jumpers and leggings. The more we talked the more a cloud began to lift; I started to realize you could do both, be an attentive mother and get back some sense of yourself. Though this lady seemed like she never lost it. I also got the sense she probably still had sex with her partner and actually liked it and she didn't look tired either.

I decided to pluck up the courage to see if she wanted to swap numbers so we could go on playdates together (and become best friends and be put in a care home next to each other in later life). And then something bizarre happened.

I was wearing a dress and while we chatted an olive fell between my legs on to the floor. We both noticed it at the same time. There was a pause. I thought about saying, 'Do you have any crusty bread? We could have a picnic.' But something stopped me.

I suppose the silence came from her thinking about where the olive had actually fallen from. I mumbled about the deli but she wasn't listening. Olive gate.

I looked at her; she looked at the olive on the floor. We looked over at our children playing sweetly.

'I think it might rain today, you know,' she said.

'Yeah, it will do, I've left my washing out,' I replied (a lie, but how do you say, 'Look, that olive didn't fall from my vagina'?).

'Right, I think it's lunchtime, Betty,' she said to her daughter.

I grimaced to myself as I wondered if that had made her hungry. Oh no, I realized, she's trying to get away from me.

'Lovely to meet you,' I said.

'Yeah, you too!'

And like that she was gone. Out of my life for good.

Or was she?

This morning, something miraculous happened and then something quite tragic. Actually, perhaps tragic is a bit dramatic – 'mortifying' is the right word. I think it's worth adding that I have not exaggerated in any way. As with everything else here, this is as it really happened.

Not wanting to be beaten and still feeling very isolated and lonely in some ways, and wanting to bond with other mums who complement my perception of myself at this particular time, I took Elsie and toddled off to a morning playgroup. This one was in Hebden Bridge. I've been a couple of times but thought we'd try it again.

It's a fair walk that involves cutting through the park, and we walked past so much rubbish left by the teenagers the night before. Elsie had just watched the *Peppa Pig* episode about recycling – except of course it's not about recycling, it's a fable about letting a small pig rule a loveless marriage, a father who comfort eats and a mother who's addicted to gambling on her laptop. There's a reason the grandparents live up such a big hill too…

Anyway, my daughter shouted out, 'Look, Mummy, litter! How naughty. Oh no, it's all over the floor!'

I was so upset for her; it felt like her first taste of injustice, apart from when her spaghetti hoops are too close to her potato waffles. I jumped to the rescue and put all the lager cans and cider bottles underneath the pushchair to take to the recycling bins.

The first set of bins were full to the brim but we would pass some more so we hoofed off. Elsie noticed some wonderful socialist graffiti on the wall: 'Eat the Rich', with a picture of the earth with blood pouring out of it. Next thing we know, the cutest puppy bounded over. We played with it, with its proud owner beaming, then we passed the café that does wonderful cheese toasties and we were first in line as it opened. The assistant stopped to chat and tell me how cute my child was.

I suddenly realized that time was getting away and I ran with the pushchair to the play group. I have never been early or on time for playgroup and I really wanted to get my £1.50-worth this time. As we rushed in, lo and behold, who did we see? The mum from the park yesterday! My buddy!! I then remembered about the olive.

'I'm so sorry about yesterday!' I said to her.

'Oh, what about?'

'The olive that fell out of my dress.'

'Don't worry, it happens to me all the time, bits of food and stuff.'

I thought that it didn't really but we laughed anyway. I could tell she was the type of woman whose sink was never blocked with bits of food but who also wouldn't judge you if your sink smelled of egg. She had lovely teeth.

'Oh yeah,' I said, 'I once went for a walk and a slice of mushroom fell out of my sleeve and I hadn't even been cooking with mushrooms.'

She looked confused...then her eyes widened and she laughed a huge laugh, her eyes filled with kindness. I imagined us all on holiday together – my husband and her husband manning the barbecue, the kids playing together in the pool. In this fantasy, my legs were as long as hers and I was good at maths and I could drive.*

The playgroup was so much fun, Elsie played happily with... what's her name? The other child...and me and the mum talked about music and art and TV and silly accidents we'd had.

When it was time to leave, the other mum helped me down the outside steps with the pushchair. I'd ignored the sign that said we were meant to leave them outside. As we carried it I finally plucked up the courage to ask her if she wanted to swap numbers. But as I did she seemed a bit distracted, like she wasn't listening. I followed her gaze and soon realized she was looking at A MASSIVE PILE OF LAGER CANS AND CIDER BOTTLES UNDER MY PUSHCHAIR!

'They're not mine, I got them from the park...I write for Radio 4!'

---

* Jon – Does Kevin (or whatever this fictional prick's name is) know that we don't eat meat? I know this is just a fantasy but I don't want you all to be having a great time while I'm having an argument for the third time that week about how most of the soy that is grown on the planet is used to feed cattle, not humans.

It was no use.

Such a shame that we will have to move to a different town. And there is such a lovely deli here.

HEIGHT OF TIREDNESS

My dad is up visiting and has taken Elsie for a walk in her pushchair. I asked him to walk on pavements in a straight line and to not cross any roads. When he gets to a dead end, he is to start over again, backwards and forwards until she has napped for 45 minutes.

I explained why it is really important that when she is asleep he must not, under any circumstances, stop the pushchair. I made it clear that if he stops the pushchair the baby will wake up and once she is awake it is impossible to get her back to sleep. She sees it merely as a disco nap before a big rave. What will then happen is she will need a catch-up nap around 5pm and then this will make her too wide awake to sleep at a decent bedtime time.

(My editor informed me in his notes that you don't say 'bedtime time'. He wrote: *Nobody says 'bedtime time', it's already done for you with the 'bedtime' bit.* He is of course wrong, despite being a parent himself. It is very important to put 'bedtime time' because she has a 'bedtime' and then she has a time she wants to go to bed, and they are different. 'Bedtime' does not usually include when she falls to sleep. It is a series of activities and sometimes it's more of a concept for me, really. It's a set of events that comfort only me. It's like levels in a game and I stick to them, I take her through each one but only SHE, this small, beautiful child, will ultimately decide the pace, the degree of resistance and the moment of eventual surrender at the end.)

Anyway, as I said to my dad, 'A late bedtime time will mean she crashes out instead of drifting off to sleep, this will then mean she wakes several times in the night, which will affect my mental well-being the next day.' My dad nodded and left quietly.

I had 45 minutes to shower, answer emails, relax, wash the pots, possibly nap…instead I got all my old photos out of the loft to see if I was cuter than my own child when I was a baby.

My hunch was correct! I was cuter! This wasn't actually anything to do with quality genes, which I must add we have given to my baby in abundance, including blue eyes and dimples, which I don't have. I was cuter due to that chubby squashed-cheek look. My baby is a wonderful body weight – those lovely chubby thighs and chubby feet, her beautiful round cheeks and belly – but the chub I was owning can't be re-created with Ella's Kitchen and a weekly organic veg box. My chub was made by 1980s sausage rolls. I mean, we know what sausage rolls are like now, so god only knows what they put in them in the eighties. Actually, even God wouldn't know what they used to put in twentieth-century meat-based pastry products.

What was lovely about looking through my old photographs was all the memories that came flooding back. The eighties now seem like a film, really. In many of the photos I'm sat with people that have passed on. It's like it all belonged to another world.

I pine a bit that I can't bring up my daughter in the world of those photographs. I can't shake off how odd it seems that so many of the people who loved and protected me aren't here to see my child grow up. I've got such an urge to take her to my grandad's house when my granny was alive, to set her down next to 'Mother' – our nickname for my great grandmother – and Arthur, her boyfriend.

It's Christmas with them all that I'm yearning for, the room thick with smoke from Silk Cut cigs, Mother's little Yorkshire terrier with bits of food mangled in its fur beard. Arthur was a cook on the trawlers in his heyday and he'd get up early and make 'breadcakes'. They're bread rolls, basically, for anyone outside of the Hull region, but honestly, hand on heart, you've never smelled or tasted anything so delicious. I loved to watch his big tattooed arms and gold-coined fingers buttering them. I was never up early enough to see him make the dough but the smell wafting around my grandad's bungalow would wake me. I know I said custard was love but these breadcakes were unconditional love. We think about great authors or musicians leaving behind a body of work but Arthur's breadcakes will be forever praised and remembered in our family.

I miss the way my granny laughed; I want Elsie to see it. As I'm writing this, big daft tears are falling from my face – I'm a bit overwhelmed with sadness and happiness that I got to experience that 'full house' feeling: all the matriarchs and the junior matriarchs, four generations of women and the sense of safety and well-being that it brought. Did they know back then how special that was? I hope so.

My granny didn't laugh out loud but she was the one you noticed the most; she'd shake and weep silently, having to wipe her eyes from under her thick brown 1980s glasses, her beautiful thick and curly hair bobbing up and down. It would make us all laugh how much it pained her to laugh!

I had a strong bond with my granny and my grandad too. I think they were, in the early days, like parents, as I lived with them for a number of years, the formative years. I seem to know a lot of people who spent a number of years living with grandparents. I think, despite the reasons for it, which are often a bit traumatic, you can develop a sort of old-fashioned quality to your nature because of it. Not that they were old (they will have been in their late forties then!). You can get a sort of sense of calm from spending your time with people who have already gone through the process of raising a child and they are likely to be set to just enjoy every minute of your company. My granny and grandad were both born on Hessle Road, a fishing community in Hull, their dads were trawler men and sea faring ran as far back in their families as anyone can remember, back to the days of whaling. My grandad did such a good job of keeping the stories and traditions alive, taking me to the docks. He was and is a storyteller and is the reason I do what I do for a living, no doubt about it.

While I was growing up, my granny and grandad were both art teachers, living on a friendly cul-de-sac in a pretty little village. I could go in and out of the houses of most of the neighbours, who I adored, and there was a jumble sale every Sunday at the bottom of the street. I'd go for walks with my grandad and come home to a lovely stew cooked by my granny. It was idyllic, but it was normal to me then and it set me up to carry such a sense of happiness with me.

I never got the feeling that my life with my grandparents (after about age five I spent my weekends and holidays with them) overshadowed my own parents, who divorced when I was two. It supported them. I can still remember how it felt when my granny picked me up and danced with me in the living room; her voice was deep, a bit out of tune, but I could hear her heartbeat. Another time, I crawled onto her lap at some sort of function above a pub, the music vibrating through the chair. I fell asleep with the sound of her humming, gently tapping my back in time with the music. Gosh, it hurts to write it, it hurts from a deep place. Doesn't it seem so unfair that someone you share such a strong connection with, who represents a sense of safety, can be taken away from you?

The feeling of grief passes over me quickly as I think of my mum and my aunt and uncle – granny was their mum and I think of how it must feel for them. I still have a loving mum and dad, of course. Looking at Elsie keeps reminding me of the love I've received.

I'm able to pass this on – this sense of love and safety, the dancing slowly in the kitchen cheek to cheek, the humming and patting to sleep, the sense of closeness I had – I'm able to pass this on to my child. Our home is a happy home and she feels safe and I thank God for that, I really do.

I forgot to tell you what happened when my dad got back from the walk yesterday.

He came striding back with the pushchair (with Elsie in it) and he seemed really pleased with himself.

'Thanks Dad, where are her shoes?' I asked.

'She didn't have any on,' he said.

I mean, she did, but never mind.

'Lucy, forget about that,' my dad said. 'Look at this! Look at her face when I do this.'

My dad bent down and shouted 'ARSE' in my daughter's face, like a foghorn. Elsie basically pissed herself laughing – a deep, hoarse laugh like she'd been propping up the bar all day in a pub in Morecambe.

'That's great Dad, thanks.'*

DANNY D-LOCK

The other thing that was in the box of the photos I've been looking at the last few days was a leavers' book from high school. I say 'leavers' book', that makes it sound professional. It's an exercise book that everyone scribbled in. I hadn't seen it for years and I forgot how feral our year group was. On the front, I said I was 'buzzin' and someone has asked 'Do you like big fat dicks?'

The book constantly refers to a party I had. I'd forgotten that a large proportion of my year group had turned up to my tiny two-up, two-down house when I was trying to give my best friend Claire a small surprise party while my mum was away. The house was trashed, utterly trashed, though in a friendly way. Someone brought a 'For Sale' sign into the house while very drunk; a head was dunked in Claire's cake; the police turned up and someone stole my iron.

I was so touched by the so-called 'bad lad' who came over the next morning and helped me tidy up. I'll never forget you, Liam. I think maybe Liam might have had a bad-ass mum like mine.

---

* Jon – This would be about the time you were teaching her to say 'bugger', I assume? 'Arse' has very much been a gateway drug where swearing is concerned and Elsie's language means most of what she says could not be broadcast before her own bedtime.

Nevertheless, it felt special that a lad who was seen at school as a tearaway was the only boy to come and help me.*

Here's the two most prominent things I remember about my high school:

1 A new boy called Danny started school. During the first hour following his arrival, someone put a D-lock around his neck. The teachers had to search everyone for the key. From that day on, he became known as Danny D-lock. Danny wrote a lovely message in my leavers' book about a fond memory he had of 'getting off' with my friend while I was in the bedroom with them fighting with a blow-up alien.

2 The only 'famous person' we ever had visiting our school was two young guys from a local radio station. They did a talk about chlamydia. A girl sitting next to me was upset that she now knew what it meant as she'd been going to call her child it.

---

* Jon - I, too, would like to thank Liam for kickstarting your interest in men who despite being unashamed 'bad lads' nevertheless have a compulsion to tidy up. Anyone doubting my 'bad lad' credentials should note I once found a bulb of garlic in my trolley in a supermarket car park that I had forgotten to put on the conveyor belt and thus had not paid for. I did NOT go back inside and resolve the issue as I wanted to be home in time for *Countdown*. That was the sweetest homemade curry I ever had, I'll tell you. I'm not naming the supermarket or the time because even though I am a bad lad they can solve crimes from the past in all sorts of ways these days and I don't want to get busted into the slammer now I've gone straight. I've got kids, man.

MUM FRIENDS

I've found a lovely Catholic playgroup and, like most faith playgroups and church schools, most people who go aren't that religious. The mums at this group are great laugh; we've formed a little group due to us somehow sensing that we all find it acceptable to drink gin on a playdate. I look forward to seeing them, which is lovely. And do you know what else is nice? Bumping into them when you walk down a street. Oh, how I've longed to 'bump into' people. I'm a very good bumper into-er. I know how to crack a few jokes and throw in one that's a bit risqué as you walk away so you both leave laughing. No matter what mood I'm in, I've always got time to bump into someone and have a natter. Jon hates the idea of bumping into someone and having to talk shit to them, pardon my French. I think that's why we suit each other – he has no choice when he's with me.

But thank goodness I have finally made some mum friends! I don't know what I was worried about. We're in a WhatsApp group together and the banter is great; they're just a lovely down-to-earth, non-judgemental bunch of mums. All of us know our bodies have lost it and many of the mums are clearly still in baby-making mode – broody northern women who like to have a drink and a laugh and don't take parenting too seriously, apart from me. But I like that I'm the anxious one, the one with my 'London ways'.

We decided to go to a nightclub last night. We went for a meal in Manchester and then to a late-night bar and then we all said fuck it, let's go dancing. Inside, it looked like a youth club disco and we felt like we were part of the PTA and had volunteered to come and keep an eye on everyone.

I headed straight to the toilets, past a diamanté camel and a neon sign saying 'sex sells'. I'd bought a silver eyeliner from Boots in the train station on the way, in a last-minute attempt to make me look 15 years younger. I tried to apply it while sweaty girls with limp hair and tiny waists knocked into me. I wanted to scream, 'None of you are cool! I was once cool!'

'Excuse me?' asked a girl with a henna tattoo and ten pairs of fake eyelashes. 'Have you got any deodorant?'

She thought I was a fucking toilet attendant! I nearly died.

I did the only thing I could do without telling her she didn't look old enough to need it: I ignored her and stormed out.

I kept thinking of all the things I wanted her to know. I needed her to know that I was once so much cooler than her and tell her, 'I've slept with more guitar players than you've had Yorkshire puddings, sweetheart.'

What was weird was that as I headed back over to the mums, to the group I belonged to, I spotted a few young men in their early twenties. I noticed them because a) they actually looked older than the rest of the kids in the club and b) they would have totally been my type when I was their age. Of course, they didn't look at me, they didn't notice me; in fact, they looked through me. I was invisible to them. Don't get me wrong, I wasn't wanting to flirt with them or approach them – I'm not weird and I'm happily married. It wasn't about that; it was more like muscle memory. The last time I was in a nightclub young men like those young men would have looked at me. I tried to work out how I felt about it. Mostly it felt a relief – thank God all that's over with. Let's face it, women can pay a lot of money to still have young men look at them. Just look at Amanda Holden.

The mums were awkwardly trying to dance to a beat that was in time with a spin dryer. They'd bought me a cocktail that tasted like that banana medicine they gave you as a child. Everyone in this place was a child! I wanted to grab one of them and tell them about the all-nighters I'd had, the time I stole a Henry Hoover from a service station, the music festivals, the philosophical chats I'd had with strangers in the days when drugs were pure, the hard liquor I'd drunk, the sunsets I'd seen.

These kids in this club weren't thinkers or creative, they weren't fascinated by knowledge. They needed a muse and they aren't going to find one on Instagram! Oh God, I thought, what will become of the future of culture!

These mums might look frumpy, they might not know their

Emins from their Warhols, their Velvet Underground from their Cocteau Twins, but they were children of the nineties like me and even bad nineties music was better than this rubbish! And you couldn't escape the sound of the Stone Roses and Oasis and Blur, even if it wasn't for you at the time, even if you liked the band Steps, which was basically just music for ice arenas. We were spoilt. Brit pop exploded in our ears, Labour was in power, we ate the rich, we, we…

One of the mums broke my train of thought: 'My husband said he's got a boner. I might go home and see if he's still up for it.'

Oh God. I turned to the meek one of the group, needing some comfort. She said, 'Gosh, it's past ten o'clock. I hope I can still make it to afternoon tea with my aunt tomorrow.'

I was about to ask her what her favourite cake was when a young boy in tight white trousers, no socks and loafers shimmied over with his back to us. He farted and then shuffled back to his sixth-former mates. The smell was foul; we all grimaced. One mum out of nowhere did a slut drop and we all had to help her up. Then the lad came back, just as we were all bent over. He dropped another fart and went back again. I couldn't believe it, I saw red! I marched over, tapped him on the shoulder and shouted, 'YOU NEED A POO, GO TO THE TOILET!'

We left shortly after that.

TERRIBLE TWOS

So here we are, bang in the middle of the two-year mark. I honestly don't think it's been that bad! She does less 'meltdown' and more 'lining up'. What I mean by that is she likes to line objects up – she'll make such a long line, it can run the full length of the house! She'll do it with things out of the kitchen cupboards and I can't stop her really; it's like a mission and the concentration on her face is very intense. I don't know how long I'm meant to leave her 'lined-up stuff' out for. I'm used to getting a saucepan off the floor now (and cleaning it) rather than looking for it in the cupboard. She did it with all the dog bowls in the pet section of the garden centre the other day. The manager came over, I think to tell me to stop her (it was a bit of a hazard) but when he looked closer he could see she was doing it with such precision he didn't want to interfere. We both just watched her, like two apes watching a human open a tin of beans or something.

LITTLE MAM SYNDROME

You know how I said things were going well? The meltdowns have started. Usually when she's tired or hungry or cold or hot or you've moved a building block an inch or you've not let her stand in the middle of the road or jump off a high fence. Sometimes it's if her beans touch her waffles. It causes arguments between Jon and I, just snippy little arguments, where I feel like I'm not being a good enough parent or vice versa. It makes me want to drink a lot of wine. It makes me feel on guard, waiting for the next eruption.

It's also made me write a short story, a pocket book. I thought it could be sold in every shop in the UK in the hope it might reach out to mothers like me.

THE STORY

Michelle wanted a non-judgemental child who would think she has good taste; her husband Dave wanted a pub in his garage. They always thought they'd be good at parenting because they like going to bed at 9.30 and sleeping for 12 hours.

When their bundle of joy was born, Michelle's husband looked as white as a sheet for five months. People kept asking if he was okay and he said he was but he and Michelle both knew that when she went into labour he left her to buy a four-man tent off the internet.

Larry is three-and-a-half years old. Michelle and Dave were 31 and 33 respectively when they had Larry. They are now both in their early fifties.

One day, they were all out walking in the rain. It was seven degrees and blowing a gale and they were freezing. Larry asked for an ice cream. His dad said, 'No Larry.' Larry said, 'Okay, Daddy-o, no problemo.' Larry said this in an American accent because he watches Netflix. Dave laughed.

The next day, Michelle was on her own with Larry; the weather was still damp and cold and Larry asked for an ice cream. Michelle said, 'No, Larry.' Larry screamed in her face and tried to kick a duck.

Michelle talked to the frog that she keeps in her pocket for reassurance. 'What is he doing?' Michelle asked.

'He's taking the piss out of you, Michelle, that's what,' said the frog.

Later that evening, Dave came in and said, 'Larry, turn off the TV, it's time to go to bed.' Larry said, 'Okay Dad, no problem,' and he rushed upstairs happily.

The next night, Larry's mum said, 'Come on Larry, bedtime.' Larry threw himself on the floor; his snot and tears made a pool of hate and anger on the new Ikea rug which was bright yellow (a bold choice but Michelle needed something to brighten things up. It reminded her of a time she went out with a tiny handbag and matching underwear).

Michelle talked to her frog again. 'Do you think he has a dairy allergy?'

'Oh yeah,' said the frog. 'It's called taking the piss, Michelle.'

One day, Larry and his mum were having such a great time that she hadn't scrolled through Twitter for at least an hour. They were in fits of giggles and Michelle's soul felt happy. In that moment, there was no place she'd rather be. She whispered a thank you in case there was a God as this child in front of her was made of pure light and love and surely heaven sent.

She dished out Larry's beans on toast on his preferred plate EXACTLY the way his dad does. Larry went absolutely batshit: the beans were touching the toast and he had a full-on turbo-charged meltdown.

Michelle asked her little frog, 'Is it because I'm the mother and he feels more secure to let his real feelings out?'

'No, he's a little pisstaker,' said the frog.

It was Saturday morning. Larry was going to his first birthday party in the afternoon. Dave said to Larry, 'Come on son, get in the car.' Larry jumped up, popped his shoes on and got in the car. Off they went to a petrol station to buy a last-minute present for a child at nursery that they'd never met. The child was called Denim.

Dave had decided that Michelle would take Larry to the party. Michelle doesn't yet know that by agreeing to this she will have to take Larry to every party for the next ten years. Dave will sit and look at pictures of rock climbing; he'd like to go rock climbing but he never will.*

Michelle preferred to look at photos on Facebook of her ex-boyfriend; the urge to look at an image of a human being she once had control over was very strong.

It was time for the crap party.

'Get in the car, darling,' said Michelle.

Larry looked at Michelle as if she had wiped her fresh, warm faeces all over his Spiderman outfit, wailed like a banshee and threw his shoe at her.

'Why is he doing that?' she asked her frog.

'Michelle, will you get a grip love,' said the frog. 'He's taking the mick out of you, mate, and he's got weird eyes.'

'Do you think he has too much sugar?'

'Bloody hell!' said the frog.

Dave huffed at Michelle when he saw the commotion.

'Can you get Larry in the car?' Michelle asked Dave.

---

* Jon – It's kayaking, not rock climbing, that I – sorry, 'Dave' – wants to get into.

Dave tutted. 'Do I have to do everything?'

Michelle ran off to have a cry.

'They both think I'm a failure,' she said to her frog.

'Do you like riddles?' asked the frog.

'No,' said Michelle.

'Well, you're going to get one,' said the frog. 'Take "iss" and put "p" in front – what have you got?'

'Piss,' said Michelle.

'Yeah, truckloads of it, mate.'

Michelle got invited to be maid of honour for her friend's wedding. She had a speech prepared but she was so tired and angry that it began with, 'There are people dying, wars being fought, families being torn apart, but you just enjoy yourselves.'

She never saw that friend again.

A mum friend from nursery invited Michelle on a girls' night out. They went to a nightclub and were the only women over the age 21. A young man kept coming close to them, farting and then shimmying away. He did it three times until Michelle went over to him and screamed, 'YOU NEED A POO, GO TO THE TOILET!'

She asked her frog, 'Did I overreact?'

'No, he was taking the piss to be fair, Michelle.'

Eventually, Michelle lost her frog as she was drinking too much gin. She went on a girls' holiday with middle-aged women she hardly knew and met someone called Glen. They opened up a cocktail bar in Swindon.

THREE YEARS OLD

We have reached birthday number three. Again, I tried to keep it slick, easy, not too many people. We went to a big indoor trampoline place with just a handful of well-behaved children. They were served chips and nuggets by three teenagers in the café who were nice lads, I think, perhaps saving up for tickets for a heavy metal festival. One girl worked there too, who they obviously all fancied. When they turned the lights off to bring the cake out (even though it didn't make it dark) I noticed them all looking at her. I think she liked footballers instead, or 'bad boys'. I wanted to take them aside and say, 'Look, lads, women like that don't age well. Pick a little goth girl who has four cats and sits at home writing poetry about death. She will eventually turn out to be the more interesting one.'

Oh yeah, the party went really well – no washing up, my grandad wasn't forced into a corner, I didn't have to meet nine generations of the builder's family. Sweet. But we did have to stop singing 'Happy Birthday' halfway through again, when her little lip started to wobble. I STILL FEEL TERRIBLE!

TV SHOWS

Right. We are out of the Elmo phase; our child is branching out. Over the past year and a half, I've spent a LOT of time watching kids' television. And I've started to see through the cracks! I've now worked out what they're actually all about, what they mean and who they're really for.

The amateur in this field might think that there's nothing much to see here. And they would be wrong! Here is my guide to the what's really going on in the most-watched programmes.

In a nutshell, they're all messed up.

Drum roll...

PEPPA PIG

We've all heard the rumours that this is about overbearing females. It is in many ways a study of middle-class helicopter parenting. It highlights some control issues that the mother and daughter both have. Yes, it's true that the mother fat shames the dad all the time but it's hard for her when she's working from home on a 1970s-style computer but he has a car that is fully electric.

I've realized there's a reason the grandparents live on a steep hill. They weren't ready to have grandchildren and they think their daughter should have married 'up'. They need to stop taking their kids to Italy as it's making them precocious. They need a fortnight at Butlins in Skegness, that'll stop them answering back.

This show is for families that buy a baby an encyclopaedia but then wince when their child tells a stranger's child that their dinosaur is actually a stegosaur.*

IN THE NIGHT GARDEN

A bit like *The Magic Roundabout*, this programme was dreamed up by someone who went to Glastonbury and intended to just drink cider but eventually caved in and took a substance given to them by a naked old man with a long beard who lived in a tree. They then went on a 48-hour bender and questioned everything. At some point, to help them finally sleep, in someone else's tent, they pictured a soft, spongy, blue gingerbread man sailing in a boat down a river. Yes, they've ripped off *Teletubbies* with some of

* Jon – Stegosaurus!

the design visuals but the general vibe is like if a textiles class had an *Avatar* theme one week. Iggle Piggle was once a safe word used at a bondage party that a work friend invited them to.

The show is for parents who have stopped wearing underwear as they don't have time to wash any. Parenting has not come naturally to them and they are anxious and have lost touch with their friends. They love their child but the bastard won't sleep.

PAW PATROL

This is a show about dogs that worry about having small genitals so they over-compensate by giving themselves a mission they know they're going to complete because they're too kitted out with sophisticated equipment for it to go wrong. They do not stop even for five minutes and just have a nap, eat a bone or look out at a sunset – they just rub themselves next to each other and cause mayhem. They are the cartoon equivalent of those Essex lads in pink shirts going from bar to bar, not stopping all night. Just chill out, guys – experiment with each other, feel no shame and stop thinking you need to be macho. (I've gone a bit too far there, I'll admit it.)

This show is for those parents who let their young boys hang off thin branches on trees, blissfully unaware that they are causing irreparable damage to the tree because they look like they're having 'active fun'.

HEY DUGGEE

This is dope! Watch this, it's great. I haven't got a bad word to say about it. It's funny, they collect badges and you'll be shouting out lines from it. It's kind and nothing weird. It's not trying to change the world and hasn't sprung from a drug-induced coma. Nor is it harbouring resentment and complex daddy issues. Go for it.

This show is for everyone! (I really like it!)

BING

Oh God, where do I start? I hear parents say, 'We love *Bing*!' Yes, because on the surface it's a little rabbit in dungarees, so of course you love it, and it's got that really good actor doing the narration and his tone is calm and reassuring.

But it's also a bit creepy. It has the tone of a cannibal who's managed to carefully blend your liver and put it into ramekins without spilling anything. People think *Bing* is really forward thinking as all the children in it have 'guardians' who don't look like them. Flop, who is Bing's guardian, is even smaller than Bing. When you really get under the skin of the show you realize that actually the little animal children have been abducted by these other creatures who desperately wanted to know what it feels like to be a parent. They treat them well and have a genuine desire to raise them to be good people *but they must never, ever let them leave the forest.*

Also, as a side note, everything in Bing's world is soft and padded and, as we know, the real world has sharp objects and pointy angles. There are no mirrors in this world so the child-animals never know they are different to their 'guardians'. They manage to keep up the pretence of this being a lovable kids show, apart from the episode where Bing suffocates a butterfly in his hand and, instead of sending him to see a specialist, they rub his nose in it and make him feel even worse than the voices in his head are.

This show is for anyone who has thought Hannibal Lecter would be a good dinner guest.*

GOD

I don't know what it is about living up here, near the Pennines, in a valley, but the place sort of forces you to think.

---

* Jon – A special word here for *Bluey*, which is simply wonderful telly and a programme I watch sometimes on my own when everyone else is in bed. It's all about creative play without being preachy and is hilarious. If the team from *Bluey* are reading this and considering an episode where Bluey and Bingo meet an expat dog at school who keeps tidying up toys while they are still being played with, then drop me a line.

It's winter and it's not stopped raining for two weeks straight. I've made some lovely friends now but sometimes you don't want to bombard them; sometimes with a little nipper you just need to find something to do quickly, without organizing it on WhatsApp.

We went out for a walk around the village on Sunday and the heavens opened! Really opened. We went past a little church and a service was taking place so we headed inside. I'd thought about finding God again and this was of course one of his many homes. I'm not sure if he was in or if he was at one of his more upmarket properties like the Vatican. If I was God I'd probably be in a little church on the island of St Lucia rather than one in drizzly West Yorkshire but hey, he's God, isn't he? He can be everywhere at once.

The congregation was 'older' and the church wasn't very full. The organist was just how I like them – out of tune and smiley. The vicar had a hearing aid and was talking quietly into a microphone that wasn't turned on. There was that lovely damp woody smell mixed with a faint whiff of Estée Lauder perfume and, dare I say it, urine. Yes, I've said it. Only faintly though. It wasn't unpleasant, like the base note of a very expensive perfume. It was comforting, it was the smell of the Church of England, my people.

I don't know if we take little churches a bit for granted? My love of visiting churches comes from my mum. She likes to go in them, she likes the energy, stepping into a different world and a different structure. I had the pleasure of being invited along to a gospel church in Peckham in south London once. For me, you felt everyone's soul when you walked in, laid bare, raw, and you feel a vibration, it's unmistakable. I said quietly to the boyfriend who took me, 'Am I allowed to feel this? Is this for me to benefit from?'

He said, 'Yes, of course, but don't sing louder than my nanna.'

This little village church near my home also had an impact on me. It touched my heart. I was not expecting the reaction we got when we trudged in from the rain. Elsie laughed loudly – a gurgly, raspy, shrill laugh that bounced around the stone walls. The elderly congregation turned to look at her, their faces instantly brighter, their eyes sparkled. Everyone cooed and ahhhed, the eternal mother and father in them, their hearts open, ready to care. How grateful they seemed to have a toddler in the room. She was not at all a nuisance for them as we sat at the back and Elsie made funny noises, showing off for her adoring crowd, at times getting frustrated she couldn't bite the hymn book. I felt welcome.

I used to have a great relationship with God. When I was in primary school, I used to say the Lord's Prayer every night and I truly believed he listened. It was a few years later at high school that I realized the end of the Lord's Prayer isn't 'In the name of the farmer and the son and his holy goat.' The fact that no one noticed me or corrected me I think is just wonderful.*

At the end of the service, I said I'd go back again the following week and bake a sponge pudding for the church fete. I'm going to do neither of those things. I'm a terrible, terrible person.

---

* Jon – I would have, but then I am not a church goer. Though one day I will take Elsie to Elland Road and she will learn to shout, 'You shit bastard, AAARRRGGGHHH' each time there is a goal kick. Yin and yang.

PART SIX

OH MY GOSH, SHE'S GOING TO BE TALLER THAN ME

FIRST DAY OF NURSERY

The day has finally arrived: it's Elsie's first day at nursery. Don't get me wrong, I'm ready for her to be away from us for a few hours a week. I'm ready for someone with a level three in Early Years Childcare to have full responsibility for the most precious thing in my life. I'm just not very good at letting go and I know my daughter won't be either.

Although I've forced my child to stop breastfeeding by introducing Dairy Milk buttons, she likes to still be close to my boobs. I think this shows unconditional love. These boobs, these well-worn udders, have seen better days. You don't see deflated, droopy, pale boobs like mine on anything erotic. Her loyalty to my boobs reminds me of someone who has rescued a one-eyed cat with mange…

(In fact, I once rescued a cat like that but the cat was too ugly to have in the house so I set it up in a box outside the house and when I opened the curtains it looked like it was winking at me. It had massive paws and when it laid on them, it looked like it was giving me the thumbs up as if to say, 'Everything is going to be alright.' Ah, that was nice, remembering that. Oh, no, I've just remembered that a neighbour gave me raw minced beef to feed to the cat and I made a cottage pie with it instead.)

I've bought Elsie a new outfit for her first day at nursery. It's sort of not practical and also not something you'd normally dress them in for this sort of setting. I bought her a Victorian-style two piece. I want to give the impression that at all times I dress her immaculately, in the hope that they give her extra care and attention. I just want the outfit to say: 'This is not a child you should let fall over and I will be able to tell by the creases in her velvet puffy shorts.'

I'm not sure why I picked the Victorian outfit. Perhaps, after many sessions of looking into all the other weird stuff in my life, a therapist might be able to work out why I did this.

We've already had two settling-in days for nursery and today is the third one but this time we have to leave her for three hours. At the second settling-in day, when she had a massive meltdown because I had to leave the classroom for just ten minutes, the very experienced nursery nurse told me it might take her a bit longer than other kids as she'd never seen a child react so badly. What I wanted to explain is that she's very dramatic and, perhaps due to my theatrical background, passed through the DNA, she knows how to throw her voice. But also she found it very traumatic and that is why I hate myself and I know for sure she has picked up on my insecurity and anxiousness.

I still can hear in my head that weird lady at the natural parenting hotline, all those moons ago, in the early days, who told me that a baby thinks a sabre-toothed tiger is going to come and get them if you put them down. And the truth is, if I could keep her in my pocket I would, but the pocket would have to be reinforced and have lots of activities in it and central heating and a fridge and basically the pocket would need to be a house and then of course I'd need to fit into the house and also I would need to leave the house, for sanity and to earn money. Isn't that just the problem? We sometimes rely on our work to give us sanity and, of course, it rarely does.

This is how it went today:

ME:

Are you excited about your first day at nursery?

MY CHILD:

No. I don't want to go.

When she said she didn't want to go, I thought maybe she just didn't realize how lovely it will be when she draws a picture that I can put on a fridge or when she runs out of the classroom to hug me; how we'll hang up her little raincoat on her little peg or bake a cake for her little friends and they'll come to our house for tea.

I should have listened. She really meant she didn't want to go.

We decided to not overwhelm her and that I'd take her into nursery on my own while Jon waited outside. We managed after a lot of chocolate to get her in the car. She wailed all the way there.

She did turn a corner when I told her about all the cool toys that would be there but then she wailed again when I said she had to share them with 14 other children. She stopped crying when I said they were having treacle pudding for tea and cried again when I said she had to eat her fisherman's pie to get it. She then, cool as a cucumber, hopped out of the car with me, walked into nursery and charmed everyone she met, luring them into a false sense of security.

Her key worker was, I think, beguiled by her and I was almost jealous that she was going to have the pleasure of getting to know this cheeky little thunderbolt in front of us – this fiery, kind, clever, slightly eccentric little girl – even by a three-year-old's standard. She was and is everything we've put into her and then more, she has her own personality and that personality is, well, unusual.

KEY WORKER:

Let's put an animal sticker on your peg, shall we? What's your favourite animal in the whole wide world?

MY DAUGHTER:

A pig.

ME:

Are you sure it's a pig? I thought you liked elephants.

KEY WORKER:

(Anxious, speaking to me)
Yep, you wrote elephant down on the form, we've got the elephant sticker here for her.

MY DAUGHTER:
> *I like pigs.*

ME:
> *And elephants.*

MY DAUGHTER:
> *No. The only animal I like is a pig. I want a pig sticker.*

(Me and the key worker both got slightly nervous at this point, like it was our first breakfast shift at a hotel and we'd given someone kippers instead of poached eggs. I could tell she'd done a lot of low-paid service jobs like I had – you have status over no one, not even a well-spoken three-year-old dressed like a chimney sweep.)

KEY WORKER:
> *So you'd like a pig above your coat peg? Do you know, I don't think we've got a pig sticker. I've got a dog.*

DAUGHTER:
> *('That's not what I ordered, I ordered poached eggs')*
> *I want a pig.*

KEY WORKER:
> *Oh, here we go! Look, here's a pig!*

(The key worker found a sticker and placed it on her peg. It wasn't a pig, it was just a different dog sticker. 'Good luck,' I thought.)

DAUGHTER:
> *That's not a pig!! I want to go home.*

Luckily my daughter got distracted by Play-Doh. I was relieved. So far, my whole parenting career has been one long distraction technique. 'Oh no, you're lying on the ground in protest because your beans touched your fish fingers...LOOK! There's a helicopter!' I suddenly panicked when I thought about how this most likely wouldn't last. She's not always going to spot Play-Doh in a tense situation and immediately calm down. Would I have two more years, maybe?

But right now everything was fine. Elsie was enjoying pretending to play with the key worker when really she just wanted to squeeze the Play-Doh in her hands and not answer questions about what she had for breakfast.

Then it was the time for me to leave. She clung to me like a little monkey...then came the screams. I was told to go quickly to the car and not to look back. I headed towards the car but I ran back and secretly watched from the window in the corridor. They'd calmed her down! Someone else had calmed my baby down; she had to calm down without me there. I headed back to the car and got in. We said nothing.

This was the first push, the first push giving her out into the world. 'This is mine but I want you to have it too and I want to share it with you and I want you to look after it, World.'

These feelings I was having, this 'mother-ness' – I felt it every time I read any article in the paper about someone ending up in a tragic situation. I wanted to save every child, I wanted to put all the hurting children into my pocket.

'I'm not having this,' I said to Jon. 'I'm going back in.'

'I don't think you should do that.'

'Her key worker's got a *tattoo*; she needs to be somewhere more creative,' I insisted.

Jon had his head in his hands at the steering wheel.

I didn't listen. I walked back in and ran over to her. She had 'met someone', a little boy. She was sat next to him helping him to build a train. She looked up at me as if to say, 'Oh, she's here. Come running back, have you?' Then she ignored me and moved to somewhere a bit more private with the little boy.

I felt an idiot. I sort of stood there in the middle of the classroom. It was time for them to put on their little outdoor waterproof suits as they were going to forest school. I felt a total spare part as she didn't want me to help her. I was embarrassing her. She wasn't able to express it but she looked confused at me instead.

Luckily, a little girl with a hearing aid and an eye patch noticed me and took me under her wing. She instructed me to help get her shoes. It was a clever move as it turned out they weren't her shoes and she'd been trying to find a way to steal them for ages.

The kids then had to all hold on to a rope and they went outside and walked in line down the road towards a wooded area. The little girl told me where to stand and I held on to the rope too. At this point, my own child could hardly look at me as she tried to play it cool in front of her new friends. The nursery nurses didn't really address why I was coming with them, which was perhaps slightly worrying, but maybe it was because I was on telly a bit, I don't know. I must admit Jon's face, sat in the car, watching me waddle away with 14 toddlers, was a picture – he sort of did a double take.

After a while, I really started to enjoy myself. I got the ball rolling with 'Three Blind Mice', though when I got to 'cut off their tails with a carving knife' I paused, but I was too far into it so I added 'and then gave them back to them'. You forget how some of these nursery rhymes are a bit old-school.

I had a similar experience only the other day. We saw a ladybird and I said to Elsie, 'I know a song about a ladybird. It goes, "Ladybird, ladybird, fly away home, your house is on fire, your children have gone."' Elsie just sort of looked at me, with her little cherub face and enquiring eyes. I shrugged and said, 'That's what they told me.'

I really thought about it after, how times have changed since the 1980s, when the expression 'children should be seen and not heard' was still used. Regularly, when I was a child of six or seven, I'd dress up in my granny's nighties and put her false teeth in and walk in on them watching *Bullseye* and no one would bat an eyelid. I hope Elsie will be interested in my stories from my childhood. I've got a lot to tell her, like how my granny made me a three-piece suit out of the leftover curtain material but she also made cushions and a throw with the same material and so when I sat on the sofa I disappeared.

I'd like to tell her about when Nanna had her legs taken off due to gangrene and I asked if they fed her legs to hungry dogs – we laugh about that a lot as a family. There was also that time we were on a train and I was nagging that I was hungry and then a man got on the train with a machete. We all hid under the tables while the police handcuffed him and my little hand came up and I took a gentleman's sandwiches. I suppose I don't know what the moral of these stories are yet or if they should just come out of the blue? We'll have to see, something to look forward to.

Elsie and her new friends seemed to be living in a different world altogether. We came to the part of the forest school walk where the kids had to go down a little hill to get to the woods. There was lots of brambles and nettles so they were instructed to put their arms up in the air and because of their little boiler suits they looked like convicts under arrest coming out of a hostage situation – dead cute really.

I decided I should leave. I felt okay about her making a fire with 14 other children under five years of age and three nursery nurses. Mainly because the girl with the hearing aid had her shit together. She was a natural leader who had a lot of common sense. She checked I was okay as I left and I thanked her for looking out for me. I told her to stop stealing shoes and she just raised her shoulders in a sort of melancholy way, as if to say, 'That's life, kiddo, we've all got our vices.'

'I'll look after her for you,' she said to me. My heart melted. I trusted her.

I got back into the car and we waited for them to come back up the hill. I counted them to check they had them all. I counted four more than I remembered. I hoped I was wrong and they hadn't collected a group that had been left there all night from the day before or something.

Our daughter was full of it when she got back in the car – she loved it!

'Aww! Are you looking forward to going back tomorrow?' I asked.

'No,' she said.

'Tell daddy what your favourite animal is.'

'An elephant,' she replied.

I put Elsie in the bath as usual but when I placed her in the water she went sort of rigid and stared into space. Of course, my first thought was 'sepsis' as it always is when you're a first-time mother and hypochondriac. I kept saying her name; she stared at me but sort of through me. The hairs on the back of my neck stood up. My heart was racing.

'What wrong, sweetheart?' I asked, panic beginning to rise.

'You've forgotten to take my socks off, Mummy.'

WHO'S IN CHARGE?

My child woke me yesterday. I saw the darkness outside and took her back to bed; it was obviously the middle of the night. I went back to sleep. She started to sing James Brown's 'I Feel Good' and then I heard the postman arrive. 'Shit, it's not night-time, it's just November.'

I thought I liked autumn. I've been saying it for years. I've now realized I just like coats, and brown leaves.

My child woke me up again this morning while I was deep dreaming about the TV presenters Ant and Dec. I was dating one of them but he'd only let me stand on his left side so I dumped him and dated the other.

'Mummy!'

I instantly got up, not wanting to make the same mistake as yesterday. I shuffled her downstairs, answering various obscure questions involving death, ghosts and spiders. It hurt our eyes when I turned on the kitchen light. I made myself a coffee. Something felt different; it was quiet, still. We were both fairly silent. She got to it before I did.

'Is it morning, Mummy?'

'Yeah! It's just winter.'

I looked at my phone, it was 3.45am.

I am not winning at parenting.

Somehow, somewhere between putting her socks on to take her downstairs and arriving at this conclusion, she'd managed to persuade me to give her a 'smorgasbord' breakfast. Once this has happened I can't go back. This type of breakfast has to be placed on a large tray. I must, as in a Michelin-starred restaurant, dot small items of food around in some sort of pattern.

We usually run with breakfast – a bit of fruit, a yogurt, a piece of toast, some nuts – and then we enter the biscuit phase. I always say no, so she asks for a chocolate instead. I say it's not breakfast food and she reminds me that 'pain o'chocolate' has chocolate in it. I hate that she knows what pain o'chocolate* is but at this point I start to think it's all heading south anyway so I give in to her requests and then lo and behold we're on the sugar train and every 20 minutes she wants something sweet.

To some people, it will sound like I'm just rubbish with boundaries. Let me use today as an example to demonstrate how we get on this sugar train:

I really needed a wee but she was stood on my dressing gown belt and was making aggressive noises at me so I gave in and gave

---

* Jon – The famous Irish breakfast, Pain O'Chocolat. Raw plugs raw plugs raw plugs.

her the chocolate to put on the smorgasbord (a tea tray). As I was weeing, she shouted through to me that the chocolate that she's now taken OFF the board is going to be her starter. She then said she would therefore need another one to replace it on my return. I just followed her orders – they were clear, concise, said with authority. I've been programmed to follow this, haven't I? This is one of the reasons I don't hold a criminal record, I'm such a compliant member of society.

Basically, this child is holding me captive.

Then, I took the chocolate milk out of the fridge by accident. My reflexes weren't quick enough and she saw it. I don't buy this stuff for her. It's really for Jon and me to swig at witching hour, just before bedtime when you're lagging, but here it was – it was in the house, with a cartoon cow on it, loaded with sugar. It's the morning and she's already had a chocolate.

Firstly, she was very unhappy that she didn't know we had it in. 'Why didn't you tell me we had chocolate milk?' she said, in the same reproachful manner a newly wedded wife might talk to her husband following his third late night working in the office. I was put on the spot. What do you say? I said sorry to her. I poured her a glass and she drank it slowly, not taking her eyes off me. I felt the weight of the injustice she was feeling. I didn't know what her next move would be.

I think I first came up with a 'smorgasbord breakfast' to make her sit in one spot for a longer period of time than usual on one of the handful of times that I was incredibly hungover. I basically arranged lots of breakfast-type items that didn't need any cooking, alongside some snacks. I created what you might perhaps call an 'artisanal pig trough'. I didn't think that she would continue using the word 'smorgasbord'. Imagine my mother's surprise when she gave Elsie a piece of toast one morning, only to be asked, 'Where's my smorgasbord?' thereby shattering the dreams held by a northern working-class nanna in her late fifties of taking her grandchild to a run-down café for a bowl of chips and a jumbo sausage roll, with all the old dears commenting, 'Ooh, what lovely hair she's got!' as they shuffle outside for a fag. Instead, when the hard-faced but heart-of-gold waitress comes over to take the order, the golden-haired child clutching a teddy bear from the charity shop next door says, 'Do you have a smorgasbord on the menu?'

Depending on what area of the country you live in, you will think I've failed or won at parenting so far.

After the chocolate and the chocolate milk, Elsie paused, put down the glass and, with a milk moustache that she wouldn't let me wipe off, her eyes a little wider after the hit of sugar, said to me, 'I think we should do some baking.'

Oh God, oh God, those words… They make you feel it's a parent-led activity but really they just want the access to the raw egg and sugar and chocolate powder. Then they go mental around the house while you try to tidy away the chaos in the kitchen. Just when things have calmed down, the buns are ready and the cycle repeats itself. This is of course what happened to us. I explained she couldn't have a bun until after her tea but she ate one while I talked to the postman about why he no longer could bend down to put letters in the postbox.

My child was now high as a kite, like totally wired and it was only 10am.

As we know, what goes up must come down. The tears then started, on this occasion because I helped her too much with a jigsaw.

I got us out of the house quickly. We ran to the park. We reset, we had a laugh, I tired her out and got us to lunchtime.

'What do you want for lunch when we get home? A pasty or a sandwich?'

'Let me think,' she said. 'We made six buns, didn't we?'

PEASANTS

It's Christmas. We've been living in this West Yorkshire village for a year and a half and it's finally feeling like home – and by home, I mean Hull.

My little cherub has taken another leap in her development –

she's now speaking beautifully in this very eloquent voice, but she still sometimes gets the odd word wrong, which is very cute. For example, she says 'av-a-bo-bo' for avocado. We all laugh and then I feel wretched that we give her middle-class avocados! (What's happening to me?) She likes wearing dresses, even though we dress her quite tomboyish most of the time, but she's still very little and most dresses for her age bury her. (I won't buy a size smaller because, as we know, 'you'll grow into it'.)

I took her for a walk to Co-op, for which she chose to put on one of her party dresses that go down to her little chubby ankles – a little Christmas tartan number – with sparkly boots and a little handbag and fluffy coat and hat. I was a tiny bit self-conscious that she was dressed like she was going down the red carpet at the premiere of a children's film in Leicester Square and we were in Co-op in Mytholmroyd village but she 'worked it' nonetheless.

A builder covered in muck, with a hi-vis top on and his rolling tobacco hanging out of his back pocket, swaggered towards the till. He didn't notice Elsie until she looked up at him and, sounding just like a cartoon version of a very small Princess Margaret, said to him, 'Good afternoon.' The guy was totally stunned; I don't think he'd ever seen something so little speak. He looked at me and I sort of just shrugged as if to say, 'I'm sorry, we've got money but it's TV money and I did go to a local comprehensive.'

He said hello back, as if he'd bumped into his old headteacher, subconsciously feeling Elsie had some sort of status but not sure what it was. It's the same natural superiority she has over us. I think basically she's old-fashioned and you feel like she's been here before, that she can teach you something. Obviously this isn't a healthy foundation for a parent–child relationship; I'm sure she could grow up pretentious but at the moment I forgive her because she's very cute.

We went up to the till and paid for the Disney *Frozen* magazine and a Freddo. The lady behind the till adores my child. Her eyes always light up when she sees her.

'Oh, hello you, and what have you been doing today?' she asked Elsie.

Elsie looked up at her and then at me.

I said, 'Mummy's been a bit naughty and let you have some of your toys that were meant to be for Christmas Day, haven't I?'

'Yes,' said Elsie in posh little voice. 'Me and Mummy have been playing with peasants.'

'Presents,' I said. I looked at the lady and laughed but she was actually very confused. 'Presents, she means.'

'No, peasants. I've got lots of peasants at my house.'

I died for a minute because we do have a gardener.

The lady laughed a big full-bellied laugh. 'That's made my day,' she said.

A SLIPPERY VICAR

Today, spring was in the air, the sun was out and flowers were in bloom. It's nearly time for our daughter to start pre-school and we're all feeling the weight of it.

We took Elsie to a children's farm and adventure playground. I don't remember when I was kid going to such things as children's farms. I think it was called strawberry picking? We used to go to Flamingoland, which was, without sounding mean, a low-budget theme park at the time but had a zoo. Even as a small child, I didn't think the flamingos in the field blended in with the caravan park, the shell suits and the North Yorkshire setting.

This children's park we took Elsie to was posh. I know when I'm surrounded by posh people as I start to really look at them. I study them. I notice how tall the women are. We walked past the cow shed and up a ramp and, while I was thinking about all these wonderfully posh ladies around me, I turned around to shout 'MOOOO' in Jon's face to make him laugh but he wasn't there and I accidentally shouted in the face of a woman who looked a lot like Camilla Parker-Bowles.

I quickly found Jon to tell him off for not being right behind me the whole time. Then the worst thing of all happened. I was talking to a lovely vicar who was there with his grandchildren and we were discussing my faith and the day I went into the church to keep dry but then never went back. He explained that prayer can happen anywhere, a bit like you can do yoga anywhere. Then my daughter asked me to go down a big tube slide that we were standing next to. I did and halfway down I realized my blouse and bra had come undone and I couldn't slow myself down and the vicar who does yoga was at the bottom. I flashed at him and covered myself up and he walked away.

THEN of course, of course, we got in a queue to buy a furry animal from the gift shop and who should be behind me but that lady I mooed at with, yes, you guessed it, the bendy vicar. Then we saw them again at the picnic benches and then again when they looked around and I was near them at the go-karts.

We're going to Flamingoland next weekend.*

Today was a tricky rainy Sunday at home. My daughter announced at about ten to eleven that she wanted a pet wolf (I think she was hungry). I explained that it wouldn't be possible and she said that

---

* Jon – None of this would have been quite so bad had you not needed such coaxing to get into the tube slide. We had to pat you on the shoulder and tell you it would be okay in order for you to flash your breasts at that vicar. You made us all complicit. Actually, it would have been just as bad had that not been the case. But less hilarious. I have the proof on camera if anyone ever sees me at a gig and wants to see the video.

she wouldn't get dressed until she could have one.

Among the crying and lashing out, I still had time to marvel at her little button nose and dimples and realized this really is love. I had forgotten to have a wash or use the lavatory and was trying to make savoury pancakes the way she's seen a French-sounding man do it at a market in Halifax. I don't think he was actually French and I think he'd spelt 'crêpe' wrong on his van too but it still felt European because he'd given us wooden cutlery.

Jon was at the door, back home from working away. He had that disappointed look on his face that the house wasn't tidy. Not because he expected it, just because it was tidy when he left. I vented about her behaviour; he told me I should pretend I'm in control.

'Why doesn't she think I'm in control of her?' I said.

'You're not,' Jon replied.

'I know I'm not but I don't want her to think that.'

'She knows it, mate.'

That night, I went and wrote the rest of my story about Michelle and her frog – the later years.

THE STORY CONTINUED

Michelle now lives with her teenage son Larry and her new husband, Tony. She met him at a service station a couple of years ago after a glamping trip to Skipton with her husband. Her husband doesn't need a name; he didn't have an interesting thing to say in the whole of their time together – they fell in love due to mutual appreciation of Robbie Williams and hot tubs. Michelle misses her son being little; her heart aches to hold him again because he was once her cherub. Don't feel too sorry for her though, kids – she's cut off most of her friends over the years and she's bitter when anyone else is happy.

It's Monday morning. Michelle wakes up her teenage son for school with breakfast in bed. She's cut his toast the way he likes it.

'Morning, sweet pea'.

'I wish you were dead,' shouts Larry.

Luckily, Michelle has a little frog that she talks to. 'Do you think he's played too much Fortnite on his PS4?'

'No, he's taking the piss out of you, Michelle.'

That night, Michelle's husband comes home with a magazine about snowboarding. He'll never go snowboarding but he likes to pretend he's got something to look forward to. He says to his son, 'Right, time for bed.' Larry says, 'Okay, dad, love you.'

The next night, Michelle tries it: 'Larry, time for bed, son.'

Larry screams, 'Your face makes me feel sick!'

Michelle gets her frog out. 'Do you think he's got a wheat allergy?'

'He has got an allergy,' says the frog. 'It's called taking the fecking piss.'

'But is it because he feels more comfortable because I'm his mother?'

'No, he's taking the piss, Michelle.'

To cheer herself up, Michelle went to a Chippendales show at a function room behind a Toby Carvery. As Carlos jiggled his coin purse in front of her the smell of baby oil made her weep for days gone by.

Eventually, Michelle lost her frog because she was drinking too much. She went on a cheap cruise with a woman she hardly knew and met someone called Glyn. They opened up a falafel stand in a car park in Coventry and lived happily ever after.

The End.

THE DIZZY ONE

I'm not sure when the first time was that my child realized I was a bit stupid. I mean, obviously I'm not totally stupid but she's cottoned on to the fact that I'm the dizzy one out of her two parents. Sometimes she pats me on the back and says, 'There, there'. Other times I just catch a concerned look on her face. She'll notice me flapping while I search for my cash card, she'll see me put the cheese grater in the fridge or she'll watch me drop the milk.

Sometimes her reaction is more obvious, like when I put her shoes on for her and she asks her daddy if they're on the right feet.

MUMMY AND BABY MELODIES

We went to another toddler class today. She's starting to get a bit old for them and yet I'm not ready to break away. I like the routine of them, I just forget to keep going back every week. I'm still sure there's a class out there that will change both of our lives. I don't know if that's a big expectation? The class we went to yesterday was not for us, though. I should have known to stay clear of anything that has 'mummy' or 'mother' in the title. If it's a choice between 'mother and baby' and 'tumble tots', no matter what age, I should always go for the one that sounds like they're pre-empting your child falling over a lot.

Yes, we know that most classes are attended by mostly mothers but the 'mummy' ones seem more likely to be attended by the type of mother who will judge you for wearing odd socks. Some of them will need a bit longer to get used to you having an accent; others will have spent so long washing and ironing things that don't need to be washed and ironed that the fabric softener has turned their brains to mush.*

Do you know what? I'm coming out of this torturous cycle of having to pretend to be the sort of mum that they would want for a Pampers advert. The hostility and cliquiness of these types of classes should make you want to take off your nursing bra, swing it around your head and shout 'Let's all do a tequila shot!'

So, the 'Mummy and Baby Melodies' class. There was one father there. He was a very similar man to the one at the baby ballet class. I think if you introduced them to each other, like, 'Tim, this is Paul,' they'd both say, 'Oh right, yeah, we're basically the same man.' They both looked like they'd been on a hike. They most definitely have a passion for cycling and they are very tall and slender.

The father at the baby ballet class was an incredible man, so unaware and unconcerned about his own appearance and actions. At some points, I just had to sit back and marvel. He was always the first to do whatever action the ballet teacher showed us – sometimes nearly knocking over his small child to do so. He would get lost in the music, engaged in his own sensory cocoon of pretending to be a sizzling sausage in a pan or a bird flying through the sky. His floor work was wondrous. Having no spatial awareness, he wouldn't know he needed more room and mums

---

* Jon – And heaven forbid you turn up to a class as a dad! But that's for another book, I suppose, so look out for my new book due out next spring: *I Just Want to Take My Daughter Swimming, I Haven't Gone to the Lengths of Having a Baby Just So I Can Sneak to the Pool on a Wednesday Morning and Perv Over Everyone in their Swim Suits, So Please Stop Looking at Me Like That.* Just waiting on a publisher. Or anyone who gives a shit.

would have to pull their children away from his flapping feet as he pretended to be a mermaid swimming in the sea. Naughty toes and nice toes is an exercise that's clearly designed for the mums to have a bit of a breather as not much assistance is required, but he sat stretched right out on his own mat, concentrating madly, hoping, I reckon, to get some sort of certificate for his hard work.

When the class finished he'd return to loving dad mode. He'd get himself and his child a little snack out. They'd sit on a bench together and have a Ribena and some Pom Bear crisps and then he'd carefully place his child in a carrier, lace up his walking boots and off they'd go, him nodding his head at us all. What a guy! One time, his wife came instead of him. She sat on the bench the whole time and ate a very flaky sausage roll. Weird.

Mummy and Baby Melodies was bizarre though. I had to fill out an online questionnaire, then a form, then dodge several bizarre emails about merchandise, then a week-long text countdown to the class starting, and then the day arrived and I went along and it was basically just a not-very-friendly woman with a tambourine.

I was late and took my mum who didn't want to be there, hadn't had any breakfast and had a hot flush. She took off four layers of clothing and was told to put them at the back of the room, but she was told in one of those voices that's...condescending.

My mum tutted and said something like 'jumped-up Mary Poppins'. I looked to the other mums for a bit of unity but realized they were just as bad. We stuck out. My daughter was dressed in boys' dungarees and I hadn't brushed her hair.

Something started playing from the pushchair. It was a teddy that says, 'Brrr, I'm freezing.' It happened while they were pretending to be sleeping bunnies. The teacher gave me daggers and kept saying things like, 'If you were here at the beginning you'd know what to do.' I hated them all.

The little teddy also says, 'Can you put my mittens on?' but it REALLY sounds like 'Can you put my knickers on?' and it just kept saying it over and over again. The other mums (and two dads) gave me that pitying look…again.

I've been annoying Jon all weekend talking about how toxic flame retardants are and sniffing the laminate flooring for VOCs. (Don't look them up, you'll end up buying really expensive paint.) He said that he can't cope with how much I worry about things. It's funny because I think I only tell him about 2 per cent of the things I worry about.

My main worries are:
The human rights atrocities in North Korea.
Chemicals in our house contributing to indoor air pollution.
If music will ever get good again.
If the far right will take over. (I mean, even more than they already have.)

If I should stop getting highlights in my hair.

Why my pubic hair and my leg hair now meet each other in the inside, middle area of my leg.

Whether my daughter will want to be my best friend when she's older.

Oh, and the fact that she's going to start school soon.

FOURTH BIRTHDAY

Our daughter is really into *Frozen*, the Disney film,* so I thought it would be nice to get a blue cake and order an Elsa impersonator

---

* Jon – It's a small point but she's really into *Frozen 2*, not *Frozen*. She finds the original dull and the songs too emotional. I think she likes the sequel because it's more of an action film, has more jokes in it and because when you took her to the cinema to see it you both laughed because Kristoff does a silly voice throughout the film without realizing he's actually doing the voice of Sven, his reindeer. When the plot of *Frozen 2* is getting away from you it really is time to look into the long-term effects of sleep deprivation. And another small point – for anyone wondering, our daughter is named after my nanna and not the princess from *Frozen*, and yes, I am offended by the question.

to sing to her. I have not forgotten the lesson of previous years and we invited just Elsie's nanna and aunt, keeping it low key. The Elsa lady came, she was beautiful, she really was just like the real thing. Her husband dropped her off in his Ford Ka. She arrived in full costume with a mic and an amp. I eagerly went to fetch our child.

I said, 'There's a big surprise for you downstairs.' She clung to me, shaking.

'What is it?'

'It's a person,' I said.

Her eyes were full of fear. I'd made it worse.

'It's ELSA,' I said. 'ELSA'S HERE!'

My daughter couldn't take it all in, she started to cry. 'MAKE HER LEAVE.'

'But she's here to sing to you,' I said.

'I don't care, get her out of my house.'

Eventually, Elsie agreed to come to the kitchen. She had her eyes shut, chanting, 'Don't look at me or touch me.'

Elsa sang to her and she buried her head in her dad's shoulder, her nanna and Jon's sister looking on apologetically but also concerned that we were subjecting her to something she wasn't enjoying. I kept saying, 'She loves her when she's on the TV.' Jon quietly informed me that maybe the real thing was a bit different, having her in your kitchen with a microphone.

After the song finished, Elsie scuttled back upstairs, like we'd just found a mouse. Elsa was booked for two hours; we were about 40 minutes into the service – though it felt like longer. The rest of the family went upstairs too and I stayed downstairs with Elsa.

'I usually give the children tattoos now.'

Elsa gave me a tattoo, it was lovely. I took it upstairs to show my quivering child.

'Do you like it?'

'NO.'

The family all agreed that had this been a party with a lot of children and they were of junior school age it would have been lovely.

I went back downstairs and Elsa had a plan: 'I'll go into your garden and dance around outside and she can watch me from the window.'

I didn't know if this would really mess her head up or be quite magical but I agreed. I ran back upstairs and informed everyone. Jon buried his head in his hands.* Elsie wouldn't look – in a way it had made it worse – but me and Jon and his mum watched with happy, encouraging faces. She really was beautiful and even if the blonde wig wasn't right, she could really sing and she sounded like Elsa too.

'Make her leave!' our daughter shouted.

I couldn't take any more. I gave her the cash and apologized. Elsa totally understood and was very lovely. Her husband picked her up, he was just around the corner waiting anyway. Off she went.

Never meet your idols.

---

* Jon – The image of her floating around our garden smelling the flowers and dancing in the drizzle while four adults watched from an upstairs window and Elsie did Lego is one I'll never forget.

STUNNED

I put on my shoes and shouted into the living room, to Jon and my daughter, that I was going to the shops. Elsie shouted back, 'Okay, I trust you.'

I closed the front door behind me and just stood there for a moment, sort of taken aback. I went back into the house and looked at them both. Jon looked nonplussed at what she had said but I needed to know what she meant. I think she's just got a more sophisticated sense of humour than me and it was just a bit of a surreal play on words. Or she got her words wrong like a four-year-old. Or she meant it; she really trusts me to go to the shops and she's actually cut to the heart of language, what we say and what we really mean. As this is exactly what people should say to each other – not 'I love you', as that's self-centred. They *should* say, 'Okay, I trust you.'

I stood in the doorway of the living room. She had her finger in her ear and was sprawled over Jon on the sofa. 'What did you mean by that?' I asked her. She ignored me and licked her finger, then grimaced at the taste of it.

She just got her words wrong.

I knew in that moment I needed to drink more.

I bought some Ready Brek, a sliced loaf and nice bottle of pink gin. I know I need to relax more and that is exactly what I intend to do. I can feel myself tonight slowly uncoiling. We have been going to bed not worrying that a teddy will suffocate her or a soaring temperature overnight might mean we end up in A&E. Her tantrums are very easy to climb down from; she knows what she wants and she can tell me how she is feeling. We have a real laugh together. She knows how to play us off of one another – what will make us feel guilty, what will hurt, and she can turn up the dial when she wants to be adorable. She's becoming a real person – a tiny little rosy-cheeked, chubby-handed, high-pitched bubble of just pure joy. Her personality is coming out and I can see everyone she's met all rolled up into one ball. I can see how it takes a village to bring up a child.

I totally underestimated, in the early days, from birth to about 16 months, how draining it would be, and I totally underestimated what great company she would be at this age. Just not when she's hungry or tired. I feel like we're at the perfect age: when I see her profile she still looks like my little baby but we've finally pretty much cracked all the sleeping and she's more independent. I don't want these days to end, I don't want her to get any older, I don't want the outside world to seep in. But it has to, doesn't it?

Never before in my whole life have I wanted to slow down time. Okay, maybe those hazy teenage summer days, maybe that short time in my twenties in Hull, but mostly I don't stop, I keep going. She's made me stop and be in the moment, she demands it.

This age is such a gift. I don't want her to go to school, I want to give up work and get a camper van and tour the world, just us three. That's what I want right now.

Then again, it was a good bedtime tonight, it only took me 45 minutes.

Ask me tomorrow.

FOUR-NAGER

To cheer up Jon we went for a lovely Sunday family walk together and I wore a coat he bought me that I don't like and I held his hand twice.

It was nice watching our daughter run around us. I thought Jon might enjoy it because initially he did want a dog instead and it can be very similar. She said 'Woof, woof' like a dog so I picked up a stick and threw it for her but she told me to get it instead, which I did. I handed it over but she didn't want to hold it and didn't want me to put it down either so I had to carry around a mucky stick for the rest of the afternoon. This is what happens when you feel smug as a parent, it bites you in the bum.

In that moment, walking through a beautiful wood, all laughing and joking, I was also very conscious that a girl in her twenties walked past us and probably thought we looked like an ideal family. You could practically hear her ovaries click into start mode. She has no idea that our house looks like a bombsite, that we'd had an argument because I left the butter out, that my daughter still wakes up in the night quite a lot and that we hardly ever get time alone as grown-ups.

And then I stopped for just a minute, I looked at what we had and I felt overwhelmed with gratitude.

But before I could get too sentimental, a meltdown started. I'd lost the bloody stick! I tried to use a replacement but it wasn't the same; Elsie wanted HER STICK.

'HOW COULD YOU?' Elsie looked at me with UTTER contempt. 'I hate you!'

'Would you like a milky button?' I asked.

'Yes,' she said.

'I don't think that's healthy to give her chocolate every time she kicks off,' said Jon.

I wanted to run back and find that twenty-something girl. I wanted to shake her, 'Don't do it, don't do it, go and live in Berlin instead.'

SOFT PLAY

Four-year-olds are hard in some ways but, you know what, I think we've got a really brilliant four-year-old. She has fewer meltdowns and outbursts than at three years. Her speech is great. There are a few things she doesn't want to do, like go on a balance bike or stroke a horse, but that's fine. Things just seem to be flowing well. All those down days I was having and feeling guilty about having are becoming a distant memory now.

And guess what, I'm back working! A lot, not just little bits, and Jon is at home with our daughter more. I'm less in the kiddie bubble world and more in the adult world – I have my feet in both and I'm a bit wobbly, like when you get out of one pedalo boat and into another. I have also come to the conclusion that grown-up work clothes feel scratchy and it will take me a while to adjust to something that doesn't have a hood on it.

So, I've been feeling optimistic and then…

I was going to a meeting in London about some scriptwriting. Jon was away but he'd be back in time to pick Elsie up from nursery. I packed the pushchair and pushed Elsie up the hill to her nursery, the wind and rain battering down on me. She had two blankets and a hot water bottle and rain cover and some breakfast snacks; I'd basically made her a camping trip on wheels. I got the hot water bottle idea off a lovely neighbour who picks up her grandson and puts a hot water bottle on his car seat for him. She does drive a Range Rover so it's not exactly the same and, I would say, far more needed in a pushchair in the freezing cold.

I dropped her off and left the pushchair there, pretending I thought you were allowed to and hoping I'd made enough TV and radio appearances to be able to do that. Having said that, I had once been told off for using my phone in the corridor of the nursery and when I said, 'It's my agent, from London,' it didn't seem to make any difference.

Solo now, I headed to the train station and total freedom. It felt good. It was just me; things were moving on. I saw a dog, I pointed at it and said, 'Woof, woof.' The owner looked at me strangely; in fact, the dog looked at me strangely. I didn't care, I was OUT! The world was no longer a harsh and judgmental place; the *Peppa Pig* theme tune was no longer ringing in my ears.

Jon texted and said why didn't I stay over and meet some friends? YES, I could drink! Life as I knew it was BACK. I bounded up to the platform. The train was cancelled. Next one in an hour.

The café was closed. I waited an hour.

Then the next train was cancelled.

My connecting train was cancelled all day.

I went home, did the hoovering, had a sandwich and told Jon not to rush back.

I picked up Elsie from nursery. I was told off for leaving the pushchair there. Elsie was upset I didn't greet her with more snacks and that her seat was cold.

As repayment for her hardship, I took her to Playzone, an indoor petri dish of childhood bacteria that you can bounce in. As soft play goes, this is as clean as you're going to get. The 'no shoes' policy lulls you into a false sense of security but your nose…your nose knows that somewhere near the ball pool there's been an accident that's never really been dealt with fully. Like minimum wage ain't enough for disinfecting each ball and sorting out the brown stain at the bottom. Soft plays are fairly expensive places to take your child if you account for the entrance fee and the two weeks of work you'll need to take off when you all get ill.

I tried to get my daughter to play next to me independently so I could look at pictures of her on Facebook like the other mums were doing but she wasn't having any of it. She demanded I chase her to the top of the jingle jungle and then subsequently follow her pretending to be a small rabbit for 45 minutes. I was sort of happy about this because I noticed the dad sat next to me was on his iPad looking up reviews of bin liners. The other mums sat quietly on their phones looking at me like I was some kind of weirdo, letting the side down. The heat started to become overwhelming, especially once I'd climbed to the top of the maze. My child refused to take her jumper off, even though she was turning the same colour as the tomato sauce she has on her fish cakes – a sort of chemical pinky red. I'm sure they mix it with the raspberry sauce they use for their ice creams.

If you've ever wondered what sugar sounds like, go to an indoor soft play centre. A child of about seven with pink glasses and a patch over one of the lenses came to join in with us. She kept trying to pick my daughter up near the home corner and pretend they were living in a flat. When she said, 'Kids are a bloody nuisance' with my daughter on her hip and a trail of snot running down her face I almost decided that was enough and retrieved my child.

We instead played a nice game of me watching them both jump off a rubber soft-play mushroom, only to be bombarded by two brothers with wide necks and Spiderman onesies on – not appropriate dress for what is basically a huge metal box on an industrial estate with the central heating on full. I think the concept is the same as they use in dodgy nightclubs: make them really warm and they'll drink more. I was trying to keep one eye out for the boys' parents to see if they'd noticed that I had become childcare for their loud, sweaty children but I couldn't find them and I think everyone assumed that all the children were with me due to the boys having the same pinky tomato-red faces as my daughter. Perhaps they thought we were a large, free-spirited family of treehouse folk and this was how we liked to spend our leisure time.

You may think this sounds far-fetched but if you know Hebden Bridge or have even just driven through it, you'll know that it's not. There's a price to pay for living near an arty, socialist town that is actually very affluent, which is that the children are all named after planets and everywhere sells out of sourdough bread very quickly.

I've realized that I'm not ever going to be the same type of mother as my mum. I'm starting to be okay with that. I'm not a single mother who struggles to make ends meet, I'm a mother who is married to a man on the TV and I've finally become the snob I hoped to turn into. I never imagined I'd have a range cooker. I mean, there once was a time I was impressed by an extractor fan. It wasn't until my late twenties that someone introduced me to a cafetière and now we have compostable coffee pods!

I grew up wanting things very different from my mother…I have always admired Laura Ashley. I feel like Laura Ashley best depicts my soul. At a real low point for my mum financially, when I'd just started high school, my auntie paid for and helped me to decorate my bedroom in Laura Ashley flock wallpaper with a matching border and floral curtains. It was my sanctuary while the rest of the house was mid-century modern and featured retro fifties furniture from charity shops. Yes, I now realize that our house, although a bit rough around the edges, looked really cool. But I didn't want cool. I wanted to punish my mother and Laura

Ashley was the only major high-street furnishing brand that had the power to do that!

What is new information to me, though, on the snob front, is that I'm a snob who doesn't like to be around other snobs. Yes, tricky that, isn't it, but easier in some ways. I like to be the only person in Blackpool that gets an organic fruit box, that sort of thing. Luckily it means holidaying abroad is very easy. We go to Tenerife and Lanzarote and I like to dress like someone who frequents the non-touristy parts of Paris while in a karaoke bar in Los Cristianos. Also, this is brilliant as our child gets to see lots of sides of a (British) coin, if you know what I mean.

My mother was under an insurmountable amount of pressure while bringing me up, in ways we are both only really beginning to comprehend due to her recent diagnosis of adult Asperger's. We had such a brilliant, strong supportive network and I had a father who loved me very much but she was, at the end of day, a single parent and I don't think a lot of people really understand just what that is like.

What's strange for me now is bringing up a child in a way that doesn't mirror the upbringing I had. I don't have experience of living in a two-parent family, although I spent a lot of my time with my grandad and granny and I think I model them at times. What I don't have with my daughter is the 'us against the world' feeling. I don't think she'll play all the roles in a family like me and my mum did. I worry a bit that the bond isn't as strong – a bond that was forged in my case by a very early understanding that my mum found things hard and the strong desire to look after her. Although I was also an absolute twat to my mother when I was a teenager. Oh, I was awful, I know I was – answering back, rebellious, gobby…all of it.

You sometimes forget that your kids are their own people. You can see so clearly the parts of their personality that are forged from everything you've done and said and exposed them to but there's something else, something unique to only them and that's why, at the age of four, when I put my small child to bed she kissed and drew me close to her. She whispered in my ear, 'I hate you and your cooking.'

'Why?' I said.

'Too many frozen waffles.'

I thought it was hilarious!*

I think having a little girl naturally makes you think about your own mother-and-daughter relationship. So I thought I'd email my mum a list of questions – things that have happened to us in our life together or in hers that I've never fully understood. I just wanted to take the time, as an adult now and as mum myself, to dig a bit deeper. Also, if the funny and bizarre stories and memories are actually true I can pass some of them onto my daughter without worrying about perpetuating another generation of lies

---

* Jon – You never told me this! This is hilarious. The other night I put her to bed and, as I always do, I made sure the last thing she heard was me telling her that I loved her very much and to call me if she needed me. She paused for a moment and said, 'Daddy? There's a spoon in my bed.'

and half-truths! My mum seemed to quite enjoy answering my questions, I think.

Dear Mum,

Here are some famous family stories that I have questions about. Please could you give me more detail and facts about them by return.
Thanking you!

Lucy X

THE BUBBLE

Did we really see a UFO that floated in front of the window and you tried to do a kung fu kick at it?

I didn't try to do kung fu – I went into ninja mode. It's instinct when I'm protecting my own flesh and blood (you). Yes, a circular object hit the window of our upstairs flat and freaked us out. The fact it was so high shows it was flying rather than floating and it had some kind of fluid in it, so it was not a balloon as they don't float with water in them.

CATSUIT

Why did you make me visit you in a sex dungeon and fasten you into a PVC catsuit?

I was a minor celebrity in Hull at the time and maybe it went to my head but I thought I'd look good in one and I used a picture of me wearing it for my profile in my Hull Daily Mail *'Full-on, 40 and 100% Hull' column page and it was a top-secret surprise. That's why you had to come and help me.*

WOMB

You have told me and other people that I called you a taxi from the womb, is this true?

You did. It was winter, thick snow and I was heavily pregnant. I'd been to a nightclub and couldn't get a taxi. The snow was coming down hard, you were pressing down on my bladder and I was desperate for a wee. I prayed to God that a taxi would come soon. I heard you say, 'Don't worry Mummy Bunny, a taxi will be here soon.' And then one appeared. It wasn't God, it was you – or maybe a joint effort. The fact is, we got home, didn't we? Don't question a good thing.

FRIDGE MAGNET

When you first met Jon, why did you give him a figure of an ET holding a Costa del Sol fridge magnet?

Jon appreciated it and it meant he knew where he stood with me on these things.

BIRTH

Did my dad really get into a fight with grandad and did I really come home in a cardboard box that said 'Thank goodness for fresh eggs' on it?

Yes, he did. Only I think your dad was shocked because he didn't know it was my dad. (Because he'd shaved his beard off so it would grow back and be the same age as you.) He was mad because he was a day late arriving and I'd had a fit during your birth and almost bitten my tongue off and you had to be born by a suction thing attached to your head and pulled out really fast.

We didn't have anything with us to put you in because we were on holiday in Cornwall. It was an egg cardboard box that said 'Thank goodness for eggs – fresh every day'. How lovely is that? I had to sit on a rubber ring for almost 12 hours.

SPEAKING A DIFFERENT LANGUAGE

Did you really wake up speaking a different language?

Yes. I had to sleep on a camp bed in me mam and dad's bedroom right throughout puberty because of it.

BUS

Why did you turn to a woman next to you and tell her there was a pair of high heels under her bed and her husband was having an affair?

Because I had a vision.

BRICK

You wrote a play about the Krays and then in the *Hull Daily Mail* you said the mafia threw a brick through our window. Was that true or were you trying to promote the show?

Ah, no comment.

HOLE

Why did you a dig a massive hole in our garden? Did you know you'd find that huge gem stone?

Yes. How? No idea. I just knew it was there.

CUCKOO CLOCK

You told me you once had a job designing the set of *Only Fools and Horses* and that the cuckoo clock they had in their hallway came from Hull. Is that true?

Yes, but it was the hall stand not a cuckoo clock and they put the wallpaper up on the set upside down, like they do in Hull.

BRICK WALL

Did you hold up a man twice your size against a brick wall?

It wasn't a brick wall, it was an interior wall in a corridor and I held him by the neck. He was a twat, he deserved it.

CAPE

Why did you come to my graduation in a cape and fall off the stage?

I think I was a bit drunk. The cape was original 1960s and very Mary Quant. That's stylish, Lucy, so what's your problem with the cape? I don't get it.

ABDUCTED BY ALIENS

Have you really been abducted by aliens? What was in your ear? What fell out? Did the cat really disappear?

I was deaf for years in my right ear, you know this. One day, I sneezed and this thing fell out. I picked it up and it looked like a computer chip-type thing. I wrapped it in a tissue until I could find my magnifying glass and somehow dropped it. The cat ate it and disappeared for 11 days solid. I thought the cat had been abducted, not me. I've never said I've been abducted. That's our Ricky.

SCHOOL

Why did you dress up as an old woman/the Queen at school? Did you really?

Ah yes, both true, but why, I have no idea. I've blocked it out. I'm not a royalist.

STABBING

Did you really stab your brother in the back with a knife?

No. I chucked a carving knife at him. He had cut my wellies up to make inner soles for his shoes.

FITTING

At school, did you really put wet tissue over your face and pretend to have a fit?

Yes. I hated the teacher.

BIG BREAKFAST

Why did you make me go on national TV on *The Big Breakfast* and lie that I had painted a picture for a kids' competition when really it was you?

We needed a holiday, Lucy, real bad, and, okay, we only got an overnight stay but it was in a flashy London hotel, all inclusive, and you also got a new outfit and I got a leather jacket. I think maybe on some level I wanted to know if I really did look like Paula Yates.

NIGHTCLUB

Why did you take your clothes off in that nightclub just as I walked in?

I didn't! I wish you'd stop saying that! It really pisses me off, Lucy. It was JUST my top and bra, and it was for a good cause. It was to stop the record on the turntable because the DJ wouldn't play a charity single I had on me. It was just a coincidence you walked in. Anyway, I think this is why you became a comedian. On some level.

EDINBURGH

Why did you make me dress as a chip?

To promote our play Sweet UFO *and to give you a taste of what it would be like to be an actress.*

ROBBIE

Did you really meet Robbie Williams and was that really him on our answerphone?

Yes, but I regret it now, he was a twat. His eyes looked manic.

VEGAN

Did we get drugged in that vegan shop?

We did. It was the mushrooms. I was tripping all the way home.

They drugged us, Lucy; we should have gone to the police really, but I think we liked it, didn't we? I know I did. I went back to look for it a few days later but couldn't remember where it was.

THE SISTERS TWO

Did we really see two elderly twin sisters in Victorian nightdresses rise up from a canal with hair down to the floor, and why couldn't you smell them?

Let's not talk about this. I think it might be like that film Beetlejuice *where if you say 'The Sisters Two' twice they'll appear again.*

Well, I now understand far less about my mother than I did before.

Bedtime is an area she controls totally.

Elsie will allow me to take her upstairs when her TV programme has finished but once in her bedroom, we have entered an environment in which she feels thoroughly dominant. This is where the psychological warfare begins.

To begin with, she allows me to think I'm winning – she might quickly carry out one of the demands I ask of her. While keeping eye contact, she'll put on her PJs and we'll laugh and hug and sing songs. When I begin to relax, that's when things slowly start unravelling. I don't want to get cross with her, I don't want her to have to go to sleep when I've lost my temper. I hardly ever lose my temper but if I do, it happens at bedtime. I try not to, though, because I know it's me that's let her down, really – if only I could find a way for her not to take the piss.

It takes Jon about 20 minutes to put her to bed; I end up curled up with her, it's gone 9pm, my arm has gone dead and I've sung the first verse of 'You've Got a Friend in Me' 90 times. But still she doesn't drift off to sleep – no, she's so mentally tired out that she conks out. First, there's a barrage of emotional blackmail she subtly weaves in; it's tiring but she has to do it. Like how an old dame has to carry on being in the theatre as it's part of her personality. She decided at a young age she was going to be a cheeky little sod and she's stuck to it.

I know I've really lost it when we're back in the kitchen after we go past the part of bedtime where we've sung 'Twinkle, Twinkle'. This happens because she says she's very hungry or thirsty and wants to chaperone me to the kitchen. I prefer her to stay in her bed when I've been ordered downstairs but she won't because she's scared of the spider that she once saw in her room. She then usually wants to play a game on the stairs. By now, I'm so tired that I don't want to tidy up or answer emails. I'll only have the time and energy for something crap on TV. I can see in her expression, in the hint of a smirk, that she can't believe what a pushover I am.

We carry her milk and water and little snack back up,

dropping bits on the stairs. Once back in her room, she doesn't want to eat any of it and some ends up on the carpet. Then, just when she's laid in bed, quiet, calm, she tells me she needs a bedtime teddy. NOT the bedtime teddy she's already got in her bed. She's back in her domain, she's energized, she's free again and she needs to make these last few minutes count.

Now is the time to pretend the floor is lava. Yep, she adds jeopardy. Like in the final battle scene in an action movie, she goes to kick her last bit of Lego while shouting that she needs to find the right teddy. I'm distracted; she's distracted me with the teddy. Now she's fully playing with her Lego as if it's the afternoon while I'm on my hands and knees looking for a teddy we bought in Blackpool two years ago. I get the wrong teddy; I ask if it matters. It does. I find the right teddy and she gets back into bed. I stroke her face to get her to sleep. It's working! I start thinking about whether I'm going to have gin or wine and her eyes ping open… 'I NEED THE TOILET.'

We repeat, from the beginning.

TIME ALONE

Something wonderful is happening for the first time in four years. I am having three days to myself at home. I've done work stuff away but never, in all this time, have I had THREE WHOLE DAYS to myself. THREE. Two isn't enough but with three you can really reset; you can really be yourself.

Jon's taking Elsie to his mum's in the Lake District. It sounds idyllic and it is – Elsie is very lucky and Jon's mum plays for hours with her. She's calm, attentive and very centred. My mum is hyper, loud and imaginative. My mum is the bull in the china shop and Jon's mum is the person who sweeps up all the broken bits afterwards and says, 'No use worrying about spilt milk.' Basically, my child has got yin and yang grandmothers and that seems kind of cool. My mum didn't want to be called 'granny' or 'nanna', it sounded too old to her. We asked her what she wanted to be called and she said 'moo moo', on account of the fact she'd just hung up a tea towel that had a picture of a cow on it. I was relieved that was the reason. I thought it was a reference to when she made a four-and-a-half-hour recording of electro music using the noise of cows. As I said, it's yin and yang.

Elsie couldn't eat her breakfast in her excitement to leave for Cumbria – she rolled up her sleeves and darted about with the energy of a newly divorced woman happy to downsize and get away from 'that tosser' (i.e. me).

I'd laid out all her clothes on her bed and pretended it's the sort of thing I do every day, hoping that whoever designs photoshoots for the White Company catalogues (middle-class homeware store) somehow sees it and nods in approval. Sure enough, Elsie came clattering down the stars with her little suitcase and a plastic toy shopping trolley overflowing with toys. She had her sparkly handbag and was looking for Jon's car keys.

'Right, I'm ready.'

'Have you packed all your clothes I laid out?' I asked.

'I don't need any clothes,' she replied firmly.

'What's in your suitcases?'

'Teddies.'

For three days, I've enjoyed eating Marks & Spencer ready meals in front of *The One Show* and pretending I'm single.

But I've now got that pang of missing her. I just called them to hopefully hear Elsie in tears telling me she misses my silky hair and soft skin and wants to hold me close…Nope, they're in the car going for a drive because it's too wet to walk anywhere.

Elsie is crying but not because she misses me – because my phone call interrupted them listening to a song, 'Rockin' around the Christmas Tree'. I wouldn't mind but it's October.

ME:

Are you okay, Elsie?

ELSIE:

(Crying) Dad, can you put it on now?

JON:

Say hi to Mummy.

ELSIE:

(Massive breakdown) ***Put 'Rocking Around the Christmas Tree' on.***

ME:

Is she missing me?

JON:

She's emotional.

ME:

Because she's missing me?

ELSIE:

Daaaaaaad!

JON:

She doesn't want to come home, she wants to stay here.

ME:

Are you looking forward to coming home?

ELSIE:

Noooo. Dad! Whaaaaaaa.

JON:

She said she wants to stay and play with her doctor's kit.

ME:

Elsie, I've bought you a lion that's a hot water bottle.

(Silence)

JON:

She's ignoring you, see you soon.

Bloody kids.

PART SEVEN

THE GOVERNMENT ARE TAKING HER AWAY (TO SCHOOL)

HOME SCHOOL

In preparation for school, we're doing some homeschooling lessons. We don't need to of course, we're just that type of person and also she needs some structure in her day. A little bit, anyway, we think. Jon is more patient and organized so he's going to do the bulk of it while I'm working but I did some PE when he started to wither away.

He drove us to the big park so I could do my lesson. It didn't really work out, firstly because I put wellies on her for some reason and secondly because I took a rucksack full of crisps and those little biscuits you get when you have a latte in a café that thinks it's being continental by putting them on your saucer.

We got out of the car and ran across a field. Elsie fell over a mole hill and then, when she realized we weren't going to the playground, she hit the roof and demanded snacks. We sat and had them and I told her about the PE experiences I'd had, like when we went swimming with school and I wore my costume under my school uniform and forgot to take knickers in my bag for after, so I stole another girl's and have felt guilty about it for 30 years. In later life, I even attempted to track down the girl to apologize and see if she needed anything – money, therapy, a CV. Maybe she needed someone with a profession to witness a document because in the circles she has moved in since the incident, as a result of the trauma, she hasn't met anyone with the ability to hold down a full-time job.

Elsie looked at me. She had stopped being angry; I'd bored her into submission. She picked us both up, sensing just what a mess I really was.

'Come on, Mummy, let's get a McDonalds.'

THE PARTY

We've been invited to a child's birthday party by a family that is very high up in the media. I'm overjoyed – it's always good to have connections in high places, though I had made a pact with Jon that he could remove himself from any party attendances, so long as he pays me to go on behalf of him. I was really quite nervous.

We walked in and Elsie looked at me and said, 'I feel safe.'

I didn't know if she meant because she recognized some of the other children or because the family had good taste and a corner-set outdoor sofa and a pizza oven. I do think that perhaps she's inherited my snob gene. She then ignored all of the children and just wanted to play with me. I gradually coaxed her to play games with them. It was a good chance for me to meet some of the parents. I felt nervous introducing myself. I went up to the mum who had organized the party. (I couldn't find the dad, I'm sure he helped equally!) She was dressed ever so beautifully; I could tell she had an iron. My daughter came up and tugged at her sleeve as we talked.

'Excuse me?' my daughter said, in such a posh little voice, like she was in a Jane Austen adaptation. I beamed at how well we were fitting in.

'Ooh, what lovely manners,' the lady proclaimed. 'Yes, lovely?'

'Guess what my mum gives me to drink?'

'What's that then?' she said, kneeling down to her level.

'Spit.'

Elsie laughed and skipped away, leaving me to pick up the pieces.

I went bright red. I think I made it worse by blushing – of all things to say! Of course we both knew that wasn't true, but how would she know I hadn't even joked about it – what if she thought it was my northern brashness? 'I'll make yer drink yer own spit if yer not careful you little pest.'

'I think you've got another comedian in the family,' the mum said.

'Ah, phew,' I thought. It suddenly dawned on me: of course, I have nothing to worry about, everyone knows we're in show business.

What a lovely thing to realize – my daughter will get preferential treatment too!

THE IDEAL SCHOOL

We've got to start thinking about primary school because you have to apply in advance. I'm just not ready for that yet but I've been mulling it over…

I've got in my head what the perfect primary school is made up of. Basically it's the one I went to mixed up with ones I've seen in films.

This is what I'm looking for:

1 A squeaky parquet floor when you walk in and a wide hallway with pegs. (My school and in films)

An older headteacher (male or female) who is into **2** amateur dramatics and classical music but is from a working-class background. (My school)

3 A big playing field with a small hill. (My school – the dinner ladies gave us tea trays when it snowed so we could sledge down the hill)

This was my first primary. It was Roman Catholic and I was only there until I was seven. What's bizarre is that I can remember the first year of school more vividly than all the rest. My earliest memory of being at this school is when the priest came to give mass: the teachers picked out the children who weren't from a

Catholic family or likely to be getting ready for their first holy communion and made us sit at the back. I managed to steal a look at the children being blessed by a man in white clothing, taking a sip of Jesus's blood from a goblet and being given wafer bread on the tongue. I longed to taste it, longed to be a child of God, believing that the reason they didn't think I was a golden child was something to do with the fact my mum wore ripped jeans and listened to Elvis.

My second memory is of a girl with long ginger curly hair running around the playground being chased by a group of adoring boys. It stunned me and I've wanted to be of Irish descent ever since – apart from a phase I went through when I wanted to be the daughter of a Native American chief. This may have been because of the film *Pocahontas*.

My third memory is of a child coming up to me in the canteen and quietly telling me that my mother was hiding behind a bush outside. I remember it feeling like it was all happening in slow motion; even at that young age I felt sheer embarrassment that she'd do such a thing. As I looked up from my school dinner, the space around me blurred and I could feel my heartbeat in my chest. Out through the window I could see her trying to hide with a massive polka dot bow in her hair, now with bits of shrubbery in it.

I mouthed the words through the glass, 'What are you doing?' She mouthed back, 'Checking you're alright.' I mean, honestly, couldn't she just have rung the school office? (Actually, we didn't have a phone, we had to use the pay phone at the top of the street. Thinking about it, it was easier to hide behind a bush.)

Now of course, I get it. As of this week I totally get it because we are approaching the time Elsie will start education. She's of an age where there's the possibility other children might be unkind. My mum couldn't relax, she loved me and wanted to check her baby was okay – oh good grief, I'm going to do the same thing. This wasn't the only time she stalked me, by the way. The first time I got the school bus she cycled behind, waving.

The fourth-earliest memory of my school is of standing at the school gates waving at my mum to come back and pick me up. She was in a taxi and had just dropped me off and thought I was waving to say goodbye. I wasn't, it was a teacher training day, I was waving to say 'you've abandoned me by accident'.

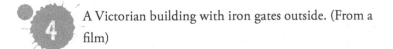 A Victorian building with iron gates outside. (From a film)

I'd really, really love it if they still have a TV in a cupboard on wheels but I imagine they won't. (My school)

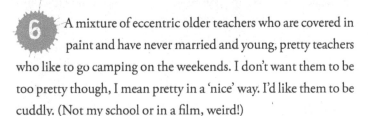 A mixture of eccentric older teachers who are covered in paint and have never married and young, pretty teachers who like to go camping on the weekends. I don't want them to be too pretty though, I mean pretty in a 'nice' way. I'd like them to be cuddly. (Not my school or in a film, weird!)

Big-breasted dinner ladies from Hull called Madge. When it starts raining, I'd like them to let the children take shelter under their bosoms. (My school, not a film)

I am now nearly almost falling asleep writing this. Some women fantasize about Tom Hardy or Idris Elba; I fantasize about 12 hours of uninterrupted sleep. I know it makes me snappy and horrible when I'm tired but anyway, as I was saying…

8 Finally, a good mixture of children, diverse. I want children from different economic backgrounds at her school.

When I was a teaching assistant, I worked in schools where nearly all the children were on free school meals and also in schools where nearly everyone was driven in by a mother in a 4x4. When a child is bored of going to Disney World you have really fucked up as a parent, I think. I'm sure the wealthier children will also contribute to society like ones from less wealthy backgrounds but, and someone needs to say it, while they're young they're just not as likeable as the children from less fortunate backgrounds. That does change but it's a fact you can't ignore. They tend to be not as imaginative, less thoughtful or not good at sharing. It's a fact even the wealthy parents can't ignore – no one likes a spoilt child, not even the parents who were once spoilt children themselves.

What we like is a child like the boy in the film *Oliver!* or the boy in *Charlie and the Chocolate Factory*. It's good to remember when we're fawning over those Instagram families in their über-tasteful Georgian terrace or country farmhouse in a Nordic-chic design, when we're thinking, 'Wow, they've got it all' – no they haven't; you wouldn't last five minutes with their kids.

This is going to be the next chapter in my baby book, it's

called 'Have I made a mistake?'

Here's how to know if you've made a mistake getting married and having children. It's also a foolproof way to see if you're going to have the type of affected children that even Nanna can't be around for too long.

1.

Have you looked at the walls in your house and thought, 'Hmm, they're too flat, they need a bit of texture, like wood panelling?'

If your answer is, 'Yes, like at Soho House, what's wrong with that?' you're going to raise a right twat and your husband is going to hate you.

If your answer is, 'No, my walls are covered in pictures my child drew and family photos' you should have two kids and live a peaceful life.

2.

Have you bought your child a toy two weeks after their birthday because you were bored and you couldn't be bothered to play with them?

You are going to raise a twat.

3.

Do you take your children skiing? This is okay in itself

BUT have you had to buy a bigger house to keep all your skiing equipment in?

You will have a twat but a good marriage; the marriage will end in divorce but it won't be too messy.

4.

Have you got a boot room with tongue and groove panelling and coat pegs and a bench?

If the answer is yes and they're also painted in Farrow & Ball colours…you're going to raise a twat.

I have noticed there are a lot of references to wood cladding having a direct effect on how you're raising your child. There is a clear link but I'm not sure who I should tell about this. I will start by telling the checkout staff in B&Q when I go to pick up some No More Nails.

I don't know whether all this is something to do with me wanting radiator cabinets and Jon thinking they're a waste of money. If you don't know what radiator cabinets are, that's a good sign really. They are little MDF covers you put over a radiator to conceal them. It also creates a little ledge along the top where you can display, oh, I don't know, ornamental frogs or something.*

---

* Jon – Why would you take the thing that heats your house and then block it from doing so with cheap MDF? That said, you never told me I would be allowed to display my ornamental frogs if we got one so let's talk.

THE STAGES

Or: 'Things My Daughter Has Been Into'

AGED ONE

Dogs that go woof woof

Chocolate

Teddies

AGED TWO

Hide and seek

Playing horsey

Chocolate

AGED THREE

Frozen* (the Disney film)

Swings

Dolls

---

* Jon – Again, *Frozen 2*.

AGED FOUR

Baking cakes

Lego

Slip roads…

Yes that's right, she's really into slip roads. She likes talking about them, identifying them, going on them. She's got her favourite slip roads and ones she'd still like to do. Nothing to worry about, I'm sure. Most of her other development changes, concerns, milestones, questions, etc., I've been able to look up on Mumsnet. Not this one sadly. Or maybe that's a good thing? Who knows where this fascination might lead. Highway maintenance? She's certainly not displaying the Greta Thunberg sense of environmentalism just yet, but that will come.

She's stopped eating meat too (I don't think it's connected). She doesn't want to eat animals, she said, but she draws the line at sausages. As she says, 'I only eat meat sausages.' She understands totally that they're made from pigs, she's seen a pig at a farm and asked if that is what they make sausages out of and we've been honest and said yes. She's then weighed up the death of the pig against the ordeal of eating vegan sausage and thought, 'Yep, I'm all in.'

As her parent, I stand by her choice and as a really bad vegan who's happy to eat her leftover sausage, I'm delighted! She tells us repeatedly that she will not eat vegan sausages and sort of drifts off and crumples up her face in disgust. She has no choice; society has forced her to do it. 'Why haven't you grown-ups invented a better meat-free sausage by now?' is what I reckon she's basically asking. And she's right, I think.

ALMOST THERE

Elsie starts school in four days.

When I talked to her about it the other day while she was playing happily in the kitchen, her little face looked up at me and she said, 'Will the other boys and girls like me, Mummy?'

If I could have picked her up and put her in my pocket and run away I would have done, but it was the first time I realized that I won't always be able to protect her, not in the moment anyway. With the skills we gave her, she will learn to adapt and navigate her way through so many complicated and confusing things, as well as so many joyful ones too.

I picked the school because the Ofsted rating was outstanding but the only thing I'm really bothered about is that the children are caring and kind. Does the school infuse this and practise and give praise for this; is it their number one priority? Nothing else matters to me now. All schools are caring places, aren't they? Or they should be. They're the most special places on earth.

FIRST DAY OF SCHOOL

Today is the day. I helped Elsie to dress and tried to act like I wasn't nervous.

As the three of us approached the door of the school, I felt my hand tighten around her little hand. We'd had the privilege of spending her first four-and-a-half years on earth cocooned in a little bubble together. I was really worried that she wouldn't want to go in, that they'd have to tear her off me, that we'd give up and go home and eat crisps and watch Netflix, cheek to cheek with a slanket on us and we'd try again next year when they would legally force me to send her to school.

The teacher opened the door and welcomed Elsie in with a big smile. Our little baby, her hair in bunches, ran in and didn't look back. No, really, I mean DID NOT LOOK BACK.

The teacher tried to get her to say bye, but she refused, metaphorically sticking two fingers up at us. She could not wait to go inside, to leave us. The teacher was slightly shocked, I think. All I could manage to say was, 'She's a character!' By this, I meant the way she talks about Halloween a lot and likes to listen to bluegrass music and can speak the English language better than most adults. But I wonder if I just came across as one of those mums who passively puts down their kids all the time. I really meant it, she's a character and they're so lucky to have her. Anyone who meets her is lucky and that's the same for all children.

Oh gosh, don't take her away from me at this golden age, every second of it needs preserving!

At the same time, I also thought, 'I'll be able to hoover in peace when I get home.'

We walked away and I turned to see her through the window. They were helping her put her little backpack on her coat peg. My eyes filled with tears. I've just left my whole world in a prefabricated building with 23 other small children who will hopefully all share a strong forest school ethos but who I hope, above all, will look after my little heart.

The second cord had been broken.

When we got home, Jon and I couldn't settle. Then the phone rang just before lunch, it was the school office. I answered it and started to look for my shoes. Jon could tell by my face – she'd obviously got too upset and needed to come home. But that was wishful thinking.

'Hello, there, we're just calling you to let you know it's all going really well and your daughter has settled in brilliantly. It's like she's always been here.'

When we went to pick her up, we were told she was a joy to be around and my heart was happy. I felt so proud!

The second day we were told that the class had looked at seeds and thought what they might grow into. They climbed a tree, collected twigs, made a den and sang songs. I asked Elsie what she did. She said, 'I ate some mash.'

The third day as we walked home from school she said she hasn't made any friends and played on her own. Just then, we turned a corner and five children ran up to her shouting her name!

The fourth day she said she was playing with a little boy she liked. I said one day he could come and play in our garden. She then said that he did a wee out of the classroom door. Jon said we'll maybe wait a while before he comes over.

And then the days after that have felt like routine. She has experiences we don't know about, faces obstacles we can't help her with. We did it. She belongs to something other than us.

THE LAST SWIG

I was working on my laptop and Jon was busy filing his tax return. I turned to him:

'Aren't things brilliant at the moment? I said.

'Yes,' he said, 'things have got easier.'

'Shall we have another one?' I asked.

'Why would you want to do that!' he exclaimed.

'Well, it's just that I've got four tins of custard left.'

ACKNOWLEDGEMENTS

I'd like to dedicate this book to my daughter Elsie. I hope she never has kids and has a nice life instead. Elsie, if you're reading this book, I'm so sorry I've detailed every embarrassing and funny moment we've had together for strangers to read. Honey, this book paid for that swing and slide set in the garden and that trip to *The Lion King* (and some of the mortgage).

Massive respect to every mother, particularly the kick-ass single ones including my mum, Gill Adams and Sarah Marshall. And thanks to my oldest friend, Claire Newlove, whose son Charlie kick-started this whole adventure by being a really cute, well-behaved three-year old.

Thank you to the amazing family I've had around me: my dad and nanna, grandad and granny, Rachel and Andy, Ricky and Mark, Mandy and Barbara.

Lastly, thank you to my doting husband, the best dad in the world x

This **monoray** book was crafted and published by
Jake Lingwood, Faye Robson, Liz Marvin, Yasia Williams,
David Eldridge, Jeremy Tilston, Marc Johns
and Allison Gonsalves.